DECATUR'S BOLD AND DARING ACT

The *Philadelphia* in Tripoli 1804

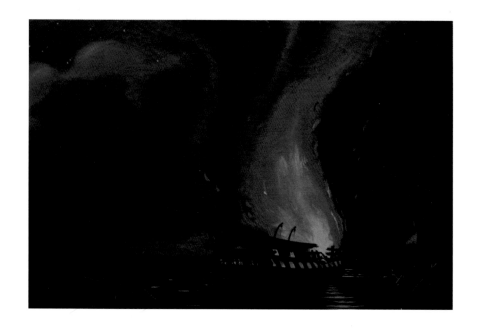

MARK LARDAS

First published in Great Britain in 2011 by Osprey Publishing,
Midland House, West Way, Botley, Oxford, OX2 0PH, UK
44–02 23rd St, Suite 219, Long Island City, NY 11101, USA

E-mail: info@ospreypublishing.com

A CIP catalog record for this book is available from the British Library

Print ISBN: 978 1 84908 374 4
PDF e-book ISBN: 978 1 84908 375 1

Page layout by Bounford.com
Index by Alan Rutter
Typeset in Sabon
Maps by Bounford.com
Art: Howard Gerrard & Alan Gilliland
BEVs: Donato Spedaliere/Alina Illustrazioni
Originated by PPS Grasmere, Leeds, UK
Printed in China through Worldprint Ltd.

11 12 13 14 15   10 9 8 7 6 5 4 3 2 1

Osprey Publishing is supporting the Woodland Trust, the UK's leading
woodland conservation charity, by funding the dedication of trees.

www.ospreypublishing.com

AUTHOR'S ACKNOWLEDGMENT

I would like to thank Bruce Biskup for making a trip to the Navy Museum in
Washington DC for me. Thanks also go to the Houston Maritime Museum –
well worth visiting if you are in the Bayou City – for their help and
assistance.

AUTHOR'S NOTE

The following abbreviations indicate the sources of the illustrations used
in this volume:

FDRL – Franklin Delano Roosevelt Presidential Library Collection
LOC – Library of Congress, Washington DC
USNH&HC – United States Navy History and Heritage Command,
     Washington DC
USNA – United States Naval Academy Collections
AC – Author's Collection
AC-HMM – Author's collection – photo taken in the Houston Maritime
     Museum
Other sources are listed in full.

CONTENTS

INTRODUCTION

For the US Navy frigate *Philadelphia*, October 31, 1803, began as another routine day off Tripoli harbor, on the North African coast in what today is Libya. The United States, at war with Tripoli since 1801, had sent squadrons annually to protect its Mediterranean shipping and blockade the city-state. *Philadelphia*, commanded by Captain William Bainbridge, was part of the 1803–04 squadron led by Commodore Edwin Preble.

The ship was one of five "subscription" frigates built for the Quasi-War with France, which was fought between 1789 and 1800. These vessels had been paid for by citizens of the cities in which they were constructed.

Philadelphia, built in its namesake city, was the largest of the five, 157ft long and 39ft wide, and displacing 1,240 tons. Rated at 44 guns, in 1804 it carried a battery of 28 18-pdr long guns and 16 32-pdr carronades. In point of fact, *Philadelphia* was smaller than the US Navy's first 44-gun frigates, including the other 44-gun frigate in that year's squadron, *Constitution*. This vessel was 175ft long, displaced 1,576 tons, and carried a main battery of 24-pdr long guns. Regardless, *Philadelphia* was larger than most European frigates, and on a par in both size and broadside with European frigates rated at 44 guns. It was a formidable warship.

As with *Constitution*, *Philadelphia*'s size and power allowed it to command the seas once away from the coast, but it was out of place in shallow waters. (*Philadelphia*'s draft was 20ft 6in aft, 18ft at the bow.) For blockade duties, Commodore Preble usually paired his frigates with a lighter warship from his squadron. The shallow-draft craft worked inshore, while the large frigate stood offshore, serving as big brother, protecting the smaller ship from Tripolitan warships if necessary. When Preble dispatched *Philadelphia* to Tripoli, the frigate was accompanied by the 14-gun schooner *Vixen*.

The two warships arrived at Tripoli on October 7, 1803, with orders to remain until November. Nearly two weeks later, on October 19, Bainbridge learned that two Tripolitan warships were already at sea, so he had dispatched *Vixen* to search for them. On October 31, *Philadelphia* was quite alone.

At 9:00am *Philadelphia*'s lookouts spotted two vessels approaching harbor. Bainbridge gave chase. Unable to draw within gunshot before the ships reached the approaches to the harbor, Bainbridge sailed in after them. American charts indicated that portion of Tripoli harbor had a depth of 40–60ft. Aware of the ship's draft and mistrusting the charts, Bainbridge's first lieutenant, David Porter, had three men at the bow, taking soundings using a lead line – a weighted line, marked with pieces of cloth tied at set intervals along the line – to measure depth.

Porter's concern was well founded. An unmarked shoal cut across *Philadelphia*'s path. The shoal lay deep – 15ft below the water's surface – but while that allowed shallow-draft craft to pass unmolested, it was much shallower than *Philadelphia*'s draft. It also rose abruptly. At 11:00am *Philadelphia*, cruising at 8 knots, sailed into these shoal waters. Before the leadsmen could give warning, *Philadelphia* moved across a submerged sand spit.

Momentum carried the ship onto the shoal. Bainbridge attempted to plow the ship forward, but this did not work. Instead, *Philadelphia* ran hard aground. Yet the stern of the ship was still afloat. If Bainbridge could lighten the ship forward, he could back the ship off the reef. This could be done by using a ship's boat to take one of *Philadelphia*'s anchors aft, and use the ship's capstan to winch the vessel back to the anchor. Under normal conditions, this procedure took routine seamanship, and both officers and crew were up to that challenge.

David Porter, shown here as a captain, was the first lieutenant of *Philadelphia* in 1804. (USNH&HC)

Conditions were anything but routine, however. *Philadelphia* was in the middle of a hostile harbor in broad daylight. It was within range of shore guns. The frigate was heeled over, obviously stuck. A Tripolitan response would soon begin, so Bainbridge and his men set to with a will, attempting to free the frigate. First to go overboard was the ship's fresh water. Consumable stores, such as food and spirits, soon joined other stores over the side. The anchors were cut away, except for one, to be used to pull the ship off the shoal. It was shifted aft, as were the ship's guns. Yet the bow stubbornly remained fixed in the sandbar. The guns soon followed most of the anchors. A few were kept to defend the ship from Tripolitan gunboats, but most went over the side.

By now it was afternoon. Initial Arab response had been desultory, but soon gunboats began approaching *Philadelphia*, like sharks circling a beached whale. While they kept their distance, they prevented

OCTOBER 31 1803

Sunset – Bainbridge surrenders *Philadelphia*

Bainbridge from employing boats to kedge *Philadelphia* off the sandbar. In desperation, Bainbridge ordered the foremast cut away. This failed to free the ship.

The gunboats had not yet attempted to board *Philadelphia*. Instead, they rowed so that they were off *Philadelphia*'s high starboard side, making it impossible for the American cannon to fire at them – the heel of the frigate's deck prevented their use. Bainbridge faced the destruction of his ship and crew and could not strike back. It was 4:00pm. The crew was exhausted by five hours of unremitting labor. Bainbridge ordered the ship scuttled. At sunset, he surrendered his frigate.

Bainbridge and the 300-plus officers and men of its crew passed into the hands of the Bashaw of Tripoli. They would serve as hostages for the rest of the war. Worse, from the perspective of the American squadron fighting Tripoli, was that the sandbar that trapped *Philadelphia* also prevented the ship from being successfully scuttled. The Arabs were able to plug the holes made by *Philadelphia*'s carpenter, and refloat the frigate. Its jettisoned guns, on the shallow sea bottom near the ship, were also soon recovered.

America's enemies were now in possession of one of the most powerful frigates in the world. If Tripoli took their prize to sea, *Philadelphia* could easily defeat six of the seven remaining warships in Preble's squadron. Only *Constitution* could match it. Preble had to retake or destroy *Philadelphia* before it could be refitted. The ship's capture that late October day put in train a series of events that would reach a climax in February 1804. The raid to destroy *Philadelphia* was a feat that Horatio Nelson, one of Britain's boldest naval commanders, would characterize as "most bold and daring act of the age."

When *Philadelphia* ran aground in Tripoli harbor on October 31, 1803, its capture created a crisis that precipitated a raid to destroy the frigate. (LOC)

ORIGINS

The conflict between Tripoli and the United States began on May 10, 1801, when Yusuf Karamanli, ruler of Tripoli, ordered the flagpole in front of the US embassy in Tripoli to be chopped down. Such an act was Tripoli's traditional means of declaring war.

Tripoli was one of what were known as the Barbary nations – a series of coastal city-states that dotted the Arab coast of North Africa. Each state – Tripoli, Algiers, Tunis, and Morocco were the principal ones – consisted of a fortified port and the coastal plains surrounding the port. Nominally all owed allegiance to the Ottoman Empire and its sultan in Constantinople. In practice, except for tribute paid annually, each behaved like a sovereign nation.

While each Barbary state received some income through agricultural products, their main industries were piracy and slavery. Their ships sought out merchant vessels of enemy nations, and seized them. Ships, cargoes, and all non-Muslims aboard the prize ship became the property of the crew that took them. (The city's ruler, of course, got a percentage of the sale of the resulting goods and chattels.) Captured individuals could obtain freedom by converting to Islam or being ransomed. Otherwise they were sold into slavery.

To keep prizes flowing, the rulers of these city-states were always at war with between one and three other nations. Europe had many small countries with mercantile fleets that plied Mediterranean waters, so the Barbary States had no shortage of victims. Nations could conclude peace treaties with the states, but these almost always included payments in cash or kind. (The treaty of amenity which the United States signed with Algiers included annual delivery of naval stores, including ship timber.)

The major European naval powers – Great Britain, France, and Spain – tolerated these antics. Barbary corsairs tended not to molest merchant ships of nations with powerful navies, unless they found these ships alone, damaged, and in a position where the capture could be plausibly denied. Britain, France, and Spain also had been fighting one another off and on over the last century. Their energies were absorbed by these wars rather than by ending Barbary banditry. Besides, the only decisive way to end Barbary

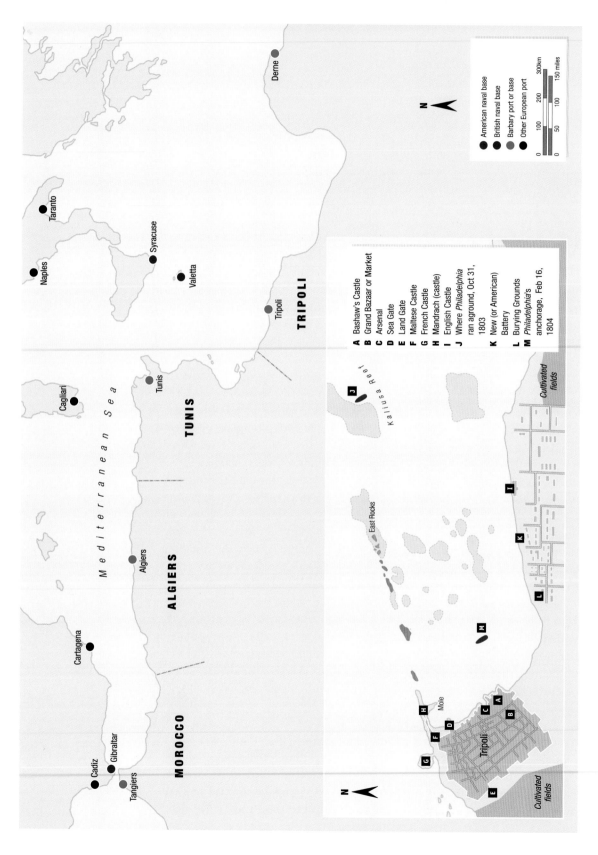

Taranto

Naples

Syracuse

Valetta

Cagliari

Tunis

TUNIS

Mediterranean Sea

Algiers

ALGIERS

Cartagena

Cadiz

Gibraltar

Tangiers

MOROCCO

Derne

Tripoli

TRIPOLI

Kaliusa Reef

East Rocks

Cultivated fields

Cultivated fields

Tripoli

Mole

N

N

American naval base
British naval base
Barbary port or base
Other European port

0   100   200   300km
0   50   100   150 miles

A Bashaw's Castle
B Grand Bazaar or Market
C Arsenal
D Sea Gate
E Land Gate
F Maltese Castle
G French Castle
H Mandrach (castle)
I English Castle
J Where *Philadelphia* ran aground, Oct 31, 1803
K New (or American) Battery
L Burying Grounds
M *Philadelphia's* anchorage, Feb 16, 1804

piracy was to occupy the ports from which the corsairs sailed. Britain, France, and Spain preferred that North Africa remain independent of Europe, rather than be occupied by rival European powers.

While the United States was a British colony, US shipping had been protected by the British flag. With American independence that protection was withdrawn, and the Barbary States cheerfully added American ships to their list of targets. At first the United States was little molested. Its trade was focused in the Atlantic, not the Mediterranean. During the period of general peace in Europe between the end of the American War of Independence (1775–83) and the start of the French Revolution (1789), Portugal kept the Barbary corsairs blockaded in the Mediterranean. Initially the United States found it cheaper to buy off the only Barbary State with an Atlantic port, Morocco.

The situation changed in 1793 when the French Wars of Revolution began, igniting 25 years of general European warfare. The war increased the demand for American merchant shipping to Europe, at both Atlantic and Mediterranean ports. Portugal abandoned its blockade of the Straits of

Ransoming of Christian captives was a major industry for the Barbary States in 1804, as it had been for centuries. (AC)

Gibraltar, allowing Mediterranean states access to the Atlantic. Eleven American merchant ships were soon taken by Algerian corsairs, with more than 100 American sailors made prisoner. In 1794, the American Congress responded by authorizing the construction of a navy.

In 1795, before the first ship of the new US Navy was completed, a peace with Algiers was signed. Naval construction stopped, with America obtaining peace through payment of tribute. Yet the price of peace kept increasing. The Barbary princes, sensing weakness, kept declaring war as a way to renegotiate peace terms. Yusuf, who had concluded treaties with the United States in 1796 and 1799, wanted more in line with those of Algiers and Tunis, when he chopped down the American flagpole in 1801. He did not realize the game had changed since 1799.

Between 1798 and 1800, the United States fought a brief and successful naval war with France in West Indian waters. The six frigates laid down under the 1794 act were by then completed, and so were seven other frigates and seven sloops-of-war. Several dozen merchant vessels were also purchased, armed, and converted into light warships. These ships were ideal for hunting down the type of craft used by Barbary corsairs.

By 1801, the United States had a navy – and was tired of constantly paying more tribute without getting real peace. When the French war concluded that year, an American naval response was possible. The American navy was downsized, but the ships sold off had been the weakest, oldest, and most useless. The remaining warships were of high quality and its officers were eager for the glory combat offered. Instead of a new treaty offer, the American response was to send a squadron of warships. Tripoli was at war with the United States – a real war.

When *Enterprise* was attacked by a Tripolitan brig, the American schooner defeated its larger, if less disciplined foe, but could not take the ship as a prize. (AC)

Yusuf was not unduly worried. The United States was a long way off – on the wrong side of an ocean. He saw war as yet another opportunity for loot, and he sent his warships out to hunt American merchant craft. He soon learned, however, that this war would differ from his earlier conflicts with the United States. His cruisers failed to capture any merchantmen because the American ships received warning of the declaration of war and cleared out of the vicinity. American naval response was prompt. The United States dispatched a squadron of four ships – three frigates, *President*, *Philadelphia*, *Essex*, and the schooner *Enterprise* – under the command of Captain Richard Dale, in June 1801. Dale was given the honorary rank of commodore – indicating that he was a captain commanding other captains.

The ships arrived in the Mediterranean in July, and soon made their presence felt. *Enterprise*, on August 1, encountered a Tripolitan cruiser, the 14-gun *Tripoli*, which thought *Enterprise* was a merchant ship and attacked her. In a three-hour fight, the 12-gun *Enterprise* battered the *Tripoli* into submission, but lacked authority to take the corsair as a prize. *Enterprise*'s captain, Lieutenant Andrew Sterett, instead dumped *Tripoli*'s artillery and small-arms overboard and forced the disarmed enemy craft to return home.

Despite the constraints on the American squadron of 1801, they served as an effective check on Tripoli. Dale had his ships aggressively patrolling the Mediterranean. He also used his frigates to protect American convoys, with the 32-gun *Essex* serving as an escort several times. Finally, he blockaded Tripoli, preventing Yusuf from using his merchant marine.

The American squadron was soon reinforced. Frigate *Boston* and sloop-of-war *George Washington* joined Dale's squadron in the fall, and the United States gained a European ally. Tripoli had declared war on Sweden, and the Swedes sent a squadron to the Mediterranean, with orders to cooperate with the American ships. By winter, Yusuf was seeking peace – or at least a truce. The United States was unwilling to include a "present" (cash) in its peace settlement. Additionally, the US envoy, William Eaton, had found a candidate to replace Yusuf as ruler of Tripoli – Hamet, a younger half-brother. Eaton wanted to play kingmaker with Hamet, hoping that a success would discourage other Barbary States from going to war with the United States. So the war continued into a second year.

The American successes in the war's first year deteriorated into a sophomore slump during the next. Dale's squadron was withdrawn in 1802, replaced by a new squadron and a new commodore. The change initiated a custom that would be followed during the rest of Barbary Wars. A new squadron of ships would be dispatched annually from the United States to the Mediterranean, and it would relieve the ships on that station when they arrived.

This system had several benefits. It kept the Navy's warships on the Mediterranean station in top condition. Sending new ships annually also ensured rotation, allowing virtually every officer in the US Navy to gain combat experience, which would prove invaluable in later conflicts. The ships sailing from the United States were freshly refitted and fully equipped when they left. Indeed, in 1802 the replacements sent – five frigates which

NOVEMBER 24
1803

Preble
informed of
Philadelphia's
loss

included *Constellation*, *Congress*, and *New York* (all rated at 36 guns and carrying a main battery of 18-pdr long guns) and light frigates *Adams and John Adams* (rated at 32 guns and carrying a 12-pdr main battery) – were far more powerful than the three frigates they replaced.

On the negative side, the policy meant that the tempo of the war could change dramatically depending upon the temperament of the captain serving as commodore. In 1802, the commodore was Richard Valentine Morris, who would prove as indolent as Dale was active. Morris was not that year's first choice to command the Mediterranean Squadron. In fact, he was the fourth. Command was first offered to pugnacious Thomas Truxton, who removed himself from consideration in a spat with the Secretary of the Navy. The Navy considered returning Richard Dale to the Mediterranean, but he chose that moment to leave the Navy due to policy disagreements with Thomas Jefferson's administration. Next on the list was Edwin Preble, but Preble was ill and unavailable. So command went to Morris.

It was a curious choice. Morris commanded the frigate *Adams* during the Quasi-War with France, performing competently, but had not been included in the original list of ten captains that the US Navy chose to retain when that war ended. He was restored to the Navy under murky circumstances, possibly due to political influence. The Mediterranean Squadron marked the first time he commanded more than a single warship.

Morris married just before receiving command. Disinclined to part from his bride, Morris applied for – and was granted – permission to take his wife and stepson on the voyage. It raised eyebrows among his fellow captains, who felt spouses at foreign stations to be a distraction.

The squadron straggled across the Atlantic, the first ship leaving in February and the last departing in August 1802. Morris's flagship, frigate *Chesapeake*, sailed in mid April. Once there, whether due to the distraction of Mrs Morris or simply Morris's preference for harbor, the squadron spent an inordinate amount of time in port. His ships underwent a leisurely refit in Gibraltar, hosted by the Royal Navy, which was curious about the American warships. He spent equally leisurely stays in Malta, Naples, and Leghorn, enjoying the hospitality of European hosts.

Morris had the authority to take, sink, or burn Tripolitan ships, an authority Dale had lacked, but failed to use it effectively. He loosened the blockade of Tripoli to the point where corsairs could slip out of Tripoli – and carry American merchant vessels back there as prizes. Finally prodded into action by frustrated and more aggressive subordinates, Morris further muddled affairs by attempting to negotiate a peace directly with Tripoli – bypassing American diplomatic personnel. His efforts only aggravated American diplomats. William Eaton, undercut by Morris and in ill-health, resigned, returning to the United States.

Morris failed as a peace negotiator. Sweden had made peace with Tripoli, leaving the United States the only nation with which Tripoli was at war. In negotiations with Morris, Yusuf demanded significantly more tribute than the year before. The demand was insultingly large, but Yusuf had only one enemy and accurately pegged his opponent as inept. War was a source of profit for Tripoli, and as long as American forces were commanded by Morris, Yusuf felt the return of remaining at war outweighed the risks it entailed.

By the spring of 1803 reports of Morris's behavior prompted the Secretary of the Navy to recall him. Orders suspending Morris were given in June, and reached the commodore on September 12, 1803. Morris was temporarily superseded by Captain John Rodgers.

A new squadron, commanded by Commodore Edwin Preble, was already on the way. In addition to Preble's flagship, *Constitution*, it consisted of *Philadelphia*, *Argus*, *Syren* (the last two were brigs, rated 16 guns) *Nautilus*, *Vixen*, and *Enterprise* (schooner-rigged and rated at 12 guns). *Enterprise*, already in the Mediterranean, was retained from Morris's squadron.

The rest of Morris's ships went home, although several officers that served with Morris managed to join Preble's squadron. Some, like Isaac Hull commanding *Enterprise*, simply remained in the Mediterranean. Others, including Stephen Decatur, David Porter, and James Lawrence, snagged commissions on ships being sent to the war. It was the only war the US Navy had at that time, and aggressive officers wanted a piece of the action.

Few of these men had previously served with Preble during the Quasi-War, but most sensed that Preble would wage a different, more active

Preble used Syracuse (labeled "Saragosa" in this period American map) as the American base of operations for actions against Tripoli. Although not as close to Tripoli as Malta, it reduced friction with the Royal Navy. (USN)

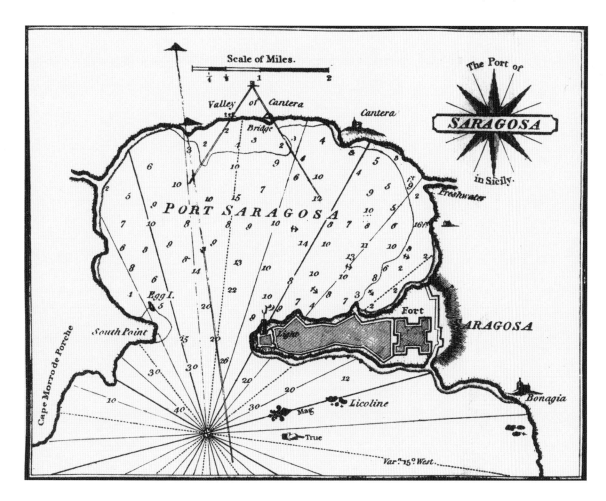

campaign than that undertaken by Morris. Preble commanded the frigate *Essex*, but spent the Quasi-War as the lone escort of a merchant convoy sailing to the East Indies. A long, difficult, independent voyage, it isolated Preble from his brother officers who served in the Caribbean. Yet Preble had carried out the mission successfully, and had the reputation of being a competent and aggressive, indeed truculent, leader.

So he would prove to be in the Mediterranean. Yet before Preble could turn to Tripoli, he had to deal with crises elsewhere on the Barbary Coast. Morocco's ruler Muley Soliman, unimpressed with Morris, sent out *Mirboka*, a 22-gun warship with instructions to prey on American merchant shipping. Preble, seconded by Bainbridge, checked Moroccan aggression. Bainbridge recaptured a brig taken prize by *Mirboka* and then captured the Moroccan warship. Preble convinced John Rodgers to delay the homeward-bound American ships long enough to join Preble's ships in a show of force at Tangiers. Intimidated, Soliman disavowed the action of his captain. Peace with Morocco re-secured, Preble moved aggressively to deal with Tripoli.

Preble chose Syracuse in Sicily as his base of operation. Malta was closer to Tripoli, but war between Britain and France had resumed in May 1803. The Royal Navy was desperate for sailors, and Preble wished to avoid the friction that would inevitably arise if US and Royal Navy warships shared a port. Preble also wanted a close blockade. With two big frigates, he planned to keep one off Tripoli at all times, backed up with one or two small warships for inshore work, while the other frigate and its companion warships refitted and re-supplied in port. The rest of the small warships would patrol independently, suppressing Tripolitan cruisers. In late September he dispatched *Philadelphia* and *Vixen* to blockade Tripoli. *Constitution* would relieve *Philadelphia* in late November – or so Preble planned.

Preble arrived in Syracuse on November 9 from Morocco, issuing a proclamation announcing the blockade of Tripoli on the 12th. He then sailed for Algiers, to land Tobias Lear, Eaton's replacement. Returning from Algiers, on November 24 Preble encountered a British frigate. Its captain informed Preble of *Philadelphia*'s loss – and reported that the frigate had been subsequently refloated by the enemy, and was anchored in Tripoli harbor. A northwest gale on November 2 had piled up water around the reef, and *Philadelphia* had floated free. A beached wooden ship is hard to scuttle, especially if labor is available to its possessor. With the labor of enough slaves, the Bashaw of Tripoli could pump water out of the frigate faster than the inflow of water through the few holes punched in its hull. The holes were plugged, and the ship towed into the inner harbor for further repair.

Seeking confirmation of the *Philadelphia*'s plight, Preble sailed for Tripoli, stopping at Malta on November 27. There, he found a letter from Bainbridge relating the story of *Philadelphia*'s capture.

INITIAL STRATEGY

Preble pieced together what had happened through a variety of sources over the next month. He received letters sent by William Bainbridge on November 1 and November 25, 1803. Reports also came in from neutral merchantmen and warships that visited Tripoli. As the situation became clearer, it was obvious that the strategic situation had become worse for the United States, yet was better than it could have been.

On the negative side was Tripoli's possession of the *Philadelphia*. Preble's squadron was down to just one frigate, *Constitution*. His enemy now possessed a warship superior to most European frigates. *Philadelphia* could fight and beat the five sloops-of-war in Preble's squadron single-handed. Reinforcements were unlikely to improve the situation. With a main battery of 18-pdr long guns, *Philadelphia* was superior to the five light frigates of the US Navy, as they carried 12-pdr batteries. Four other US Navy frigates carried 18-pdr batteries comparable to those of *Philadelphia*, but all four vessels were laid-up in the United States. Of these, *New York* and *Chesapeake* needed major refits, leaving *Congress* and *Constellation* potentially available. *Philadephia*, rated at 44 guns, was notionally superior to all of them except *Chesapeake*.

Lines of the frigate *Philadelphia*. While it only carried a main battery of 18-pdr guns, it was rated at 44 guns. (USN)

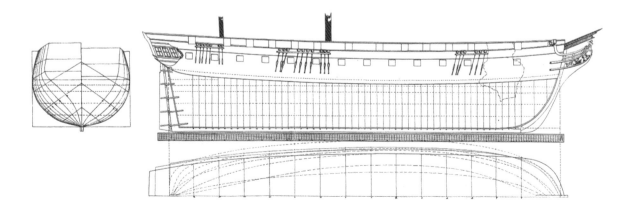

Only the three Humphreys frigates, designed to carry a main battery of 24-pdr long guns, were clearly superior to *Philadelphia*. Preble had one of these available to him – *Constitution*. The others – *United States* and *President* – were across the Atlantic, and only *President* was seaworthy. Any reinforcements, even under the best circumstances, would be unavailable until word of *Philadelphia*'s loss crossed the Atlantic to the United States, and orders were issued to fit new ships for sea duty, and the ships sailed to the Mediterranean. For the time being – most likely for the next six months – Preble's resources were the ships on hand. With the forces available to him, Preble needed to remove *Philadelphia* from Tripoli's possession. It had to be recaptured or destroyed.

Armed with one large cannon in the bow, gunboats, like the one pictured here, were formidable opponents to deep-draft warships in the sheltered waters of a harbor. Tripoli had a dozen of these craft. (AC-HMM)

The situation was not as desperate as it might first seem, however. Tripoli could not use *Philadelphia* until it was capable of taking to sea. Until then, Preble knew where the ship would be – in Tripoli harbor.

Tripoli faced several problems in fitting *Philadelphia* for sea. The first was that the Tripolitan navy had inherited what today would be termed a "bare boat." In attempting to lighten ship, the American crew had tossed overboard most of the materials needed to sail and fight a ship. The guns and the ship's anchors were scattered atop and around the sandbar on which *Philadelphia* had grounded. The ship's stores had also gone over the side. Additionally, the foremast had been cut away in the last desperate attempt to free the vessel. Everything would have to be set to rights before *Philadelphia* could again cruise as a warship.

The guns and anchors, lying in shallow water, could be recovered. Unlike their modern equivalents, smoothbore cannon and sailing-era anchors would be none the worse for immersion. But recovery would take time. An 18-pdr long gun weighed 2 tons, and salvaging them, even from a relatively shallow depth, presented difficulties. Once recovered, the guns had to be remounted. The wooden carriages on which they were mounted were likely to have been destroyed, damaged, or lost when the guns were jettisoned. New carriages would have to be built.

Refitting the hull and rearming *Philadelphia* would take months, even under the best circumstances. But there was an even bigger handicap to making the ship seaworthy – finding adequate replacements for the foremast and its spars. The various Mediterranean rigs used by the Barbary States – xebecs, tartanes, and various lateen-rigged vessels – used short masts and thin spars. These could be supplied locally. The American frigates, by contrast, required big masts and long spars. Those of American frigates like *Philadelphia* were at the limit of what was achievable with purely wooden materials. By the 19th century, the North African coast was bereft of trees capable of providing replacements. They had to be imported.

Morocco and Algiers had secured large masts from one of their few remaining sources – the pine forests of New England. Part of the negotiated payment that the United States provided to Barbary States under the peace treaties was naval stores – masts and spars. But Tripoli had been at war with the United States – which then held the same type of market power over masts that Arab nations hold over petroleum today – for nearly two years. Tripoli had a shortage of large mast timbers. That would make fitting *Philadelphia* for sea difficult.

When Preble learned of *Philadelphia*'s loss, he possessed the commodity most valuable to a commander – time to react. Word first reached Preble almost a month after the frigate's capture. It had been refloated by then, and was outfitting in the inner harbor. Although its guns had already been recovered, the ship could not sail. *Philadelphia* was useful as a harbor battery, but Preble could count on its remaining unable to sail for several months more. He had time to plan a response.

Another plus for the US Navy was that except for *Philadelphia*, Tripoli's navy was weak. Tripoli's biggest warship, *Meshuda*, was in the hands of

DECEMBER 5 1803

Bainbridge smuggles information on Tripoli's navy to Preble

Morocco, which was unlikely to return it. A second 22-gun ship had been destroyed by Morris's squadron. Tripoli was building a new 22-gun warship, but it was as unready for sea as *Philadelphia*. On December 5, 1803, Bainbridge, in a letter smuggled to Preble through the Danish consul, assessed the strength of Tripoli's navy at one polacre-rigged ship, one 14-gun brig, a ten-gun schooner (ready for launch), one xebec, five lateen-rigged galleys with four to six guns, and a dozen gunboats. The armament of the polacre was not noted by Bainbridge, but it was unlikely to have carried more than 18 guns. The xebec, polacre, brig, and schooner probably carried crews of 70–100 men each, while Bainbridge reported that the galleys had crews ranging between 50 and 60. All carried light guns – the heaviest were likely 9-pdrs, and most vessels probably carried broadsides of 4-pdr or 6-pdr long guns.

These craft were oceangoing. They were ideal for preying on merchant ships, as they were fast and carried more men than the typical merchant vessel would have aboard. The galleys were even more of a threat, as they could maneuver under oars when the winds were still, when a merchantman would be becalmed. None were capable of challenging *Constitution*. Even the small warships in Preble's squadron would likely win a single-ship action against any of these ships – and regularly had over the last two years.

The gunboats were shallow-draft harbor-defense craft. Each gunboat carried a single large gun in its bow – typically a 24-pdr long gun – and relied on oars for propulsion. The damage that this gun could do – even to a frigate – combined with a gunboat's ability to move in calm seas and over shoal waters, made them extremely effective in guarding a harbor. Seagoing sailing vessels were restricted to the deep channels, while the gunboats could cut across shallow water, and position themselves at their opponents' bow or stern out of reach of the broadside guns. In a narrow channel, the sailing ship could not even turn to fire upon the tormenting gunboat without risking running aground. Like *Philadelphia*, it would then be hopelessly trapped.

But gunboats were lightly built, and fragile. A full broadside from a schooner like *Enterprise*, with its 6-pdr guns, could sink a gunboat. A single shot from an 18-pdr – standard armament for a frigate – could break one in two. While dangerous in harbor, gunboats were unlikely to be found in open waters, and could easily be destroyed if they were found at sea.

Greater risks for the Americans came from Tripoli's formidable shore batteries. The United States believed that Tripoli's batteries might contain as many as 300 cannon. The port's fortifications actually contained only 115 cannon, distributed among 12 batteries. These were large guns. The lightest would have fired a 12lb shot. Most could shoot 24–42lb solid shot. They were protected by earth or stone embankments that the lighter guns of the American frigates and sloops-of-war could not penetrate. Finally, shore batteries had furnaces for heating shot. Red-hot shot would ignite fires on any ship struck by it. The batteries' gunners were mercenaries, who would refuse to operate the guns if they felt they were in danger, but even *Constitution*, with its battery of 24-pdr guns, would be hard-pressed to endanger the batteries' gunners.

Preble's resources to accomplish his goal of retaking or destroying *Philadelphia* were limited, yet flexible. His flagship, *Constitution*, was one of the most powerful warships in the world. Yet due to the heavy harbor defenses of Tripoli, its broadside was less useful than its crew – some 450 experienced mariners, including 25 commissioned, warrant, and petty officers. The two brigs assigned to his squadron were *Argus* and *Syren* (which was also styled "*Siren*"). These vessels were new, having been authorized in 1803. Both ships had a depth of hold of 12ft 6in, and they were each armed with 16 24-pdr carronades (short-barreled, short-range artillery) and two 12-pdr long guns. The carronades were lighter than the 6-pdr long guns similar ships would have otherwise carried, but had only two-thirds the range of the long gun. With a 94ft gun deck and a breadth of 25ft 6in, *Argus* was longer and slimmer than *Syren*. It had a gun deck 93ft 3in long and a molded beam of 27ft. *Argus* was authorized a crew of 142 men, and *Syren* 120.

Vixen was also a new ship, but it was smaller. It copied the lines of the schooner *Enterprise*, built in 1798 and widely admired for its speed; *Vixen* was a scaled-up version, as it displaced 170 tons to *Enterprise*'s 135 tons. *Nautilus*, built in 1799, but purchased by the Navy in 1803, was lighter than both at 105 tons, but was longer and wider than *Vixen*. *Nautilus* achieved this feat with its very fine hull – shaped like a concave "V" rather than the full "U" typical of that day. Each ship was rated at 12 guns, but *Vixen* had 12 18-pdr carronades and two long 9-pdr guns, while *Nautilus* carried 12 6-pdr long guns and two 12-pdr carronades. *Enterprise* mounted 12 6-pdr long guns. In November 1803, all three ships were rigged as topsail schooners, but *Nautilus* and *Vixen* would both be re-rigged as brigs during the campaign, in late 1804. Crews for the ships ranged from 70 to 111 men.

Despite these vessels, Preble lacked the naval resources to sail directly into harbor, silence the batteries, and take out *Philadelphia*. Given the strength of Tripoli's fortifications, Nelson and the Royal Navy's Mediterranean fleet – with more than a dozen ships-of-the-line – would have found the challenge daunting. While Preble's ships were excellent for their

Stephen Decatur commanded the schooner *Enterprise* when it captured *Mastico* – the ketch that became *Intrepid*. Most of the Navy personnel on the raid came from *Enterprise*. (AC)

intended mission – protecting US merchant shipping, blockading Tripoli, and chasing down Tripolitan warships – they were ill-suited for a direct assault on a fortified harbor. *Philadelphia* was sitting under the guns of Tripoli's harbor. Recovering or destroying the frigate, therefore, required the US Navy to challenge the fortifications directly.

An indirect approach was indicated – a "cutting-out" operation. A popular staple of adventure fiction writers during and since the age of fighting sail, cutting-out operations were equally beloved by ambitious young naval officers. The object was to "cut" (take) a ship out of an enemy harbor through stealth and speed. In its classic form, a party of picked sailors would row into the harbor under cover of darkness, preferably on a moonless night, in the small boats carried by a warship. Early morning – the hours before sunrise – were preferred, as the defenders would be asleep. The cutting-out party was necessarily small – limited by the number of men who could fit in three to five boats. This limit was partially due to the number of boats a warship carried, but also because the chance of detection increased exponentially as the size of the operation increased.

Success depended upon a surprise and speed. Silence during the approach was a necessity. Oars were muffled, firearms left unloaded (lest one accidentally discharged), and no talking permitted.

If the target ship was reached without incident, the cutting-out party would board the intended prize, and overwhelm the anchor watch. Were surprise total, the watch might be taken before they had a chance to rouse anyone else aboard or warn the shore. Cold steel and clubs were the raiders' preferred weapons – gunshots attracted attention. Once the raiders had control of the ship, they would set the sails, cut the mooring lines, and slip out of harbor. If all went well, with wind and tide cooperating, and no one (except the unlucky members of the anchor watch) aware that the departing ship was in enemy hands until it was well on its way out of harbor, by the time shore batteries were alerted and ready to fire the prize would be past them.

Should anything go wrong, the result could be disaster. An alerted and armed crew aboard the prize could repel the attackers before they could board – and use the ship's artillery to sink the boats carrying the party before they could withdraw. Even if the ship were successfully boarded and taken, the sounds of combat could attract undesired attention. The ship's defenders usually had loaded firearms and could use them to fight or simply to raise the alarm. Once the harbor's defenders knew that an enemy was at hand, the chances of a successful withdrawal worsened by the minute. Within an hour every battery would be on alert and ready to fire.

By 1803 the most famous cutting-out action had occurred a few years before the capture of *Philadelphia*. In 1799, Captain Edward Hamilton, then commanding the frigate HMS *Surprise*, led a cutting-out to recapture HMS *Hermione*, a British frigate seized by mutineers and surrendered to the Spanish in the Americas. Hamilton took a party of 100 sailors and Royal Marines in boats into the Spanish-held harbor, Puerto Cabello (in modern Venezuela). There they boarded the frigate, defeated a Spanish crew of 400 men aboard the ship, and sailed it out of harbor. Hamilton was knighted for the achievement.

Officers of the US Navy could not receive knighthoods, but they were aware of the opportunities offered by successfully cutting-out *Philadelphia* from Tripoli harbor. Such an operation could lead to fame and promotion – the rewards most sought by these men. All of the lieutenants serving under Preble would volunteer for the effort.

Yet with due reflection, Preble would have realized that a cutting-out operation was not the solution. The action required that the prize be sailed out of harbor. A prize crew would be hard pressed to do that successfully with *Philadelphia*, which lacked a foremast. The lost mast would not seriously handicap the speed of the frigate as it left harbor, but it would significantly restrict its maneuverability.

Philadelphia needed to thread a narrow channel to reach blue water. A full-rigged ship used sails on foremast and mizzenmast to provide leverage to turn the ship. Even a square-rigged ketch – with only a mainmast and mizzenmast – depended upon jib sails to help turn the ship. These triangular sails were set on the stays – lines running from the bowsprit and jib boom to the fore-most mast.

Stays formed one leg of a tripod of lines used to guy a mast. The other two-thirds of the tripod were formed by the shrouds and backstays. These ran behind the mast to both sides of the ship, and were set in pairs. Stays kept a mast from falling backwards. The portside shrouds kept the mast from falling forward or to the right. The starboard shrouds kept it from falling forward or to the left. On *Philadelphia*, the mainmast stays were attached to the foremast – the missing mast. With the foremast missing, there was nothing to prevent the mainmast from toppling backwards if it had sails set and the wind came from ahead of the ship – except the structural rigidity of the mainmast. This meant *Philadelphia* could not tack – swing its bow across the direction of the wind – without risking disaster. While the ship could move with just the sails on the mizzen, or after, mast, it would be difficult to hold a tight course. Without sails set in the bows to counter the leverage of

Sending sailors in small boats to capture a ship in an enemy port and sail it out was called cutting out a ship. Cutting out actions were both dangerous and glamourous. (LOC)

The principal ports used by the Barbary States were fortified harbors, giving raiding corsairs a refuge. (AC)

the mizzen sails, it was hard to control the direction in which the bow moved. Given adequate sea-room a ship could wallow out using just its mizzen sails, but in a narrow channel it would most likely ground on one of the sides.

Nor could *Philadelphia* be swiftly towed out of harbor using ships' boats or any vessel smaller than a frigate. The only frigate available, *Constitution*, could not be risked. Towing *Philadelphia* out using boats or even one of the other warships in Preble's squadron would give even the slowest gunners time to man and arm their batteries. Also, the harbor's gunboats would have time to row out to recapture *Philadelphia* and its rescuers.

By the start of December, Preble realized that *Philadelphia* would have to be destroyed. The question was how to slip a party into Tripoli harbor, destroy the frigate, and successfully escape. More specifically, the big challenge was how to achieve the first two-thirds of the objective – reach the frigate and destroy it. A successful escape was desirable, but not necessary.

THE PLAN

The plan came together in January 1804. The most certain method of destroying *Philadelphia* was to burn it. Men equipped with muscle-powered hand tools, such as axes, could only do limited damage to a frigate's hull in a short period of time. If the ship were simply sunk in harbor, it could be refloated, as it had been after it ran aground in 1803. Blowing *Philadelphia* up by carrying explosives aboard the ship was chancy. If the fuze were set for too long a time, it could be extinguished by the enemy after the boarding party evacuated. Cut the fuze too short, and the explosion would destroy the boarding party along with *Philadelphia*.

On the other hand, setting a ship on fire was simple. Fire was more feared than anything else aboard sailing ships. They were crammed with materials that did not just burn – they burned explosively. Ships were built of wood, and stuffed with canvas and cordage. The wood was seasoned – dried completely – and protected against water damage with a coat of either tar or oil-based paints and varnish. The ropes and lines were also either tarred or oiled, to preserve the line from the effects of moisture or to ensure they ran smoothly. Canvas, especially that used for partitions or as weathercloths on the ships' sides, was also oiled and painted. Even the canvas sails were carefully dried before being placed in storage (damp sails would mildew and rot). Throw in accelerants like gunpowder – every gun position would have a cartridge at hand when the guns were loaded – and you had all the elements to create a conflagration. A small fire took time to spread, but once fire took hold, it was almost impossible to extinguish. Fire would not only destroy the upper works of a ship. It would also travel downward, into the hold where high-proof spirits were stored, and into the ship's magazines. Once those were reached, the fire would grow explosively, with a force that would shatter the timbers of the hull.

Preble first mentioned the possibility of burning *Philadelphia* in a letter he sent to the Secretary of the Navy on December 10, 1803. He proposed slipping a party into Tripoli harbor to burn the ship. In the letter Preble stated he would "hazard much to destroy her." Preble was not the only

DECEMBER 10
1803

Preble first
advocates burning
Philadelphia

American naval officer to recommend burning *Philadelphia*. Its captive captain, William Bainbridge, was in secret communications with Preble. Had the American officers been released under parole as prisoners-at-large within the city of Tripoli, the officers would be honor-bound to refrain from martial activities – including espionage and escape – until properly exchanged or released at the end of hostilities. But the Bashaw of Tripoli held Bainbridge and his officers as prisoners. Bainbridge was free, therefore, to assist the American cause by any means within his power.

Bainbridge had found the means through a sympathetic Danish consul. Yusuf Karamanli needed someone to serve as an intermediary between Tripoli and the United States. Ransoms had to be negotiated. Nicholas Nissen, neutral Denmark's consul to Tripoli, served that role. Perhaps because Nissen realized that Denmark would itself eventually become the victim of Tripolitan aggression, his "neutrality" favored the prisoners. Nissen worked out a system for smuggling letters from the prison in which the captured naval officers were held. Bainbridge wrote letters using lime or lemon juice – the text dried invisibly, but became visible as brown letters when the paper on which they were written was heated. The apparently blank sheets were passed to Nissen, who forwarded them to Preble with other correspondence. They offered Preble intelligence about conditions in Tripoli, including the state of *Philadelphia*'s men and officers, and the harbor's defenses.

On December 5, 1803, Bainbridge wrote a letter to Preble advocating that a small, chartered schooner could be used to destroy *Philadelphia*. Filled with men, and commanded by determined officers, it could slip into the harbor at night, board the frigate, and burn it. On January 18, 1804, Banbridge wrote a second letter advocating an attempt to burn *Philadelphia*. In this letter, he suggested sending the party to *Philadelphia* in ship's boats.

Bainbridge forwarded both letters to Preble through Nissen. It is not clear when they reached Preble. It would have been unlikely for Preble to have received either letter before January 10, as American mail sent to and from Tripoli was routed through Malta, where it was held by the American consul there. It took a visit to Malta on January 10 before Preble learned that correspondence had been held, and the commodore was able to secure letters addressed to him and to see that the rest were forwarded to the proper recipients. Bainbridge's letters showed that different minds had reached similar conclusions about what was to be done. Besides, by January 10 a third advocate for burning *Philadelphia* had emerged: Stephen Decatur.

Decatur had been part of Morris's squadron, first lieutenant of the frigate *New York*. While in Malta he seconded a fellow officer, Midshipman Joseph Bainbridge (William's younger brother), in a duel. Midshipman Bainbridge killed his foe, a clerk in the island's civil British government. The uproar created resulted in the two being sent back to the United States.

DECEMBER 23
1803

Tripolitan ketch,
***Mastico*, captured**
and renamed
Intrepid

The imbroglio hurt neither man's career. Decatur was given *Argus*, part of Preble's squadron, despite the fact that he was one of the most junior lieutenants in the US Navy and *Argus* was the biggest lieutenant's command in Preble's squadron. Decatur sailed knowing *Argus* would be given to Lieutenant Isaac Hull, already in the Mediterranean. Decatur would in turn receive Hull's command, *Enterprise*, the smallest warship in the squadron. Bainbridge followed Decatur to *Enterprise*, and was soon rated an acting lieutenant.

The change of command proved fortunate for Decatur. *Philadelphia*'s loss made *Argus* the second-largest warship in Preble's diminished squadron. Hull was sent to the Western Mediterranean, to watch on Morocco and Algiers. Decatur and *Enterprise* moved to blockade Tripoli, the center of action.

Thus, Decatur, rather than Hull, was on the scene when *Enterprise* encountered a Tripolitan ketch, *Mastico*, on December 23, 1803. *Mastico*, flying a Turkish flag, was sailing from Tripoli to Constantinople. The ship lacked Turkish papers, and Decatur soon learned that it had come from Tripoli – indeed, it had taken part in the capture of *Philadelphia*. Loot from *Philadelphia*, including Lieutenant David Porter's uniforms, was still aboard. *Enterprise*, sailing with *Constitution*, took the prize back to the flagship. After examining the evidence – including eye-witness testimony from two men present in Tripoli harbor when *Philadelphia* was captured – Preble treated *Mastico* as a lawful prize. It was taken into the US Navy as a tender, and renamed *Intrepid*.

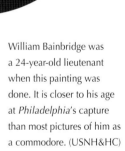

William Bainbridge was a 24-year-old lieutenant when this painting was done. It is closer to his age at *Philadelphia*'s capture than most pictures of him as a commodore. (USNH&HC)

Intrepid was a small merchant vessel, typical of the minor merchant craft in the Mediterranean. Sixty feet long, with a beam of 12ft, it displaced 64 tons. Ketch-rigged, it carried three square sails on its mainmast, with a schooner-rigged mizzen. Like most Mediterranean vessels, it was armed for protection against pirates. *Intrepid* carried four small guns, probably 4-pdrs. It was an ideal supply ship for the squadron, but Decatur had in mind other purposes – he wanted to use it to attack *Philadelphia*.

Decatur believed that he could sail into Tripoli harbor in *Intrepid*, without the ship being detected as an American vessel. *Mastico* had been a Tripolitan ship, so it was a familiar sight within the port. The American capture of the ship had not been witnessed by any other ships, and it was starting what would have been a long voyage to Constantinople. A long absence would go unremarked.

Even if it returned earlier or later than expected, those within the harbor would most likely conclude that its unexpected return was due to changed circumstances, assuming it was even recognized as the *Mastico* – it could as easily be another Mediterranean ketch, one of an anonymous multitude of small trading craft plying the Middle Sea. Decatur took the plan he formulated to Preble. Unknown to Decatur, it matched the one Preble had already conceived, and indeed, the plan en route to Preble from Bainbridge.

But Preble had not completely settled his plan. He was pondering a critical decision. Who would lead a raid? Preble was blessed with an

JANUARY 10 1804

Preble receives Bainbridge's letters advocating burning *Philadelphia*

abundance of talented subordinates. He wanted a man who was brave and competent, who believed such a plan could work, who could show independent initiative and – perhaps most importantly – balance aggression with good judgment. The choice between the right leader and the almost right leader could make the difference between success or failure. Preble now decided that Decatur was the right leader, and accepted Decatur's plan.

The plan eventually used contained several changes from Decatur's original proposal. Preble added a second ship to the expedition, the brig *Syren*. *Syren*'s commander, Lieutenant Charles Stewart, was another officer who approached Preble with a plan to burn *Philadelphia*. Stewart, returning from a cruise, spoke to Preble after Decatur. Instead of replacing Decatur with Stewart on *Intrepid*, Preble enlarged the plan, adding *Syren*.

Adding a ship increased the flexibility of the raid. *Intrepid* could be expended as a fireship, if necessary, without sacrificing its crew, which could take to the boats and be picked up by *Syren*. Without such backup they would face an open-boat voyage to Malta – nearly 200 nautical miles away – to escape the wrath of Tripoli.

Syren was also available to cover *Intrepid*'s withdrawal. *Intrepid* was a merchant vessel armed with only four light guns, vulnerable to both the gunboats in Tripoli harbor and the seagoing warships owned by Tripoli. The presence of a hostile 18-gun American brig would discourage pursuit.

Regardless of how much *Syren*'s support aided Decatur, adding *Syren* changed the dynamics of the raid. Stewart was senior to Decatur. He had been fourth lieutenant of *United States* when Mr Midshipman Decatur joined the frigate for his first cruise. Stewart and Decatur were also friends – they had known each other since childhood, when both attended Dr Abercrombie's Episcopal Academy in Philadelphia. Despite this friendship, Stewart's seniority made him superior to the independent-minded Decatur on this raid.

Preble ordered Decatur to select 63 men and five officers from the crew of *Enterprise* to man *Intrepid* during the attack. Since the adventure was both hazardous and required a high degree of personal initiative, even on

Lines of the brig *Syren*. There are no contemporary images of the brig other than this line drawing. (USN)

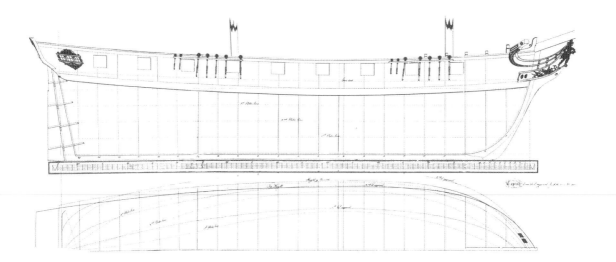

the part of the ordinary sailors, Decatur was told to take only volunteers. Preble probably intended to make up any shortfall, using volunteers from his own flagship, *Constitution*, but this proved unnecessary. Every man and officer aboard *Enterprise* volunteered. Decatur instead faced the task of pulling out a handful of men to leave behind. These would provide an anchor watch for *Enterprise*, which would remain in Syracuse harbor during the raid.

In addition to *Enterprise*'s junior lieutenants – James Lawrence, Joseph Bainbridge, and Jonathan Thorn – Decatur took the ship's surgeon, Lewis Heerman, and Midshipman Thomas Macdonough. Macdonough was intimately familiar with *Philadelphia*, having been assigned to the frigate during its cruise. When *Philadelphia* captured *Mirboka*, Macdonough had commanded the prize crew. He was at liberty because he had not been able to rejoin *Philadelphia* before the frigate ran aground.

Preble also assigned five midshipmen from *Constitution* to *Intrepid* for the expedition: Ralph Izard, John Rowe, Charles Morris, Alexander Laws, and John Davis. Preble intended to blood as many of the US Navy's young gentlemen in combat as possible. His decision gave *Intrepid* a total of 11 lieutenants and midshipmen, a ratio of one leader for every six followers.

Another important addition to *Intrepid*'s crew was Salvatore Catalano, who would act as a pilot to guide the ship in the treacherous waters of the harbor. Catalano was Sicilian, a mariner from Palermo. He had sailed into Tripoli harbor numerous times, and was familiar with its waters. On his most recent visit, while serving as master of a Maltese trading vessel sailing under the British flag, Catalano witnessed *Philadelphia*'s capture. His testimony of these events contributed to the condemnation of *Mastico*. Catalano also had no love for the Barbary States. For centuries, Palermo and communities on the Sicilian coast had been the victims of slaving raids by North African corsairs. Given an opportunity to strike a personal blow against them, he took it, eagerly volunteering for a hazardous enterprise. His knowledge, courage, and cool judgment were to be major factors in the execution of the raid.

Once the resources for the raid – in terms of ships and men – were allocated, Preble, Stewart, and Decatur developed the operational details. It was decided that once the two ships reached Tripoli, *Syren* would remain offshore, far enough from the coast that its presence could not be detected from shore. *Intrepid* would sail into harbor at dusk, as if it were a merchant vessel. The familiar appearance of the ketch would hopefully not attract attention to the ship, and approaching darkness would cloak it as it approached *Philadelphia*. The raiding party would hide below decks. A small party – consistent with the crew of a merchant ship – would remain on deck to sail the ship.

To help conceal the identity of the ship, all members of the boarding party would wear civilian clothing – the apparel consistent with that of mariners operating out of Tripoli. Common seamen in the US Navy had no uniforms. They generally wore slops – trousers, jackets, and shirts like those worn by civilian sailors. It would have been a simple matter to purchase Mediterranean-style clothing to substitute for Yankee garb.

Once in harbor, *Intrepid* would sail up to *Philadelphia*, moored in Tripoli's inner harbor, and obtain permission to tie up to the frigate. Once this was achieved, upon Decatur's command the raiders would emerge from the hold and board the frigate. In the dark it would be hard to identify friend from foe, even had the two sides worn different styles of clothing. It would be even more so with everyone dressed alike. To prevent "friendly fire," the raiders were to cry "Philadelphia" during the attack. Anyone not shouting "Philadelphia" was fair game.

There was to be no fire, friendly or otherwise, from Decatur's party. The raiders were to use only cold steel. Once the enemy sailors were swept from the deck and Decatur's party controlled the decks, Decatur would send parties below, deep into *Philadelphia*'s bow, stern, and waist, and set fires in the depth of the ship. After the fires were set and going, two of *Philadelphia*'s 18-pdr guns would be fired into the hold of the ship to punch holes in its bottom, to complete its destruction. These guns were to be positioned while the incendiary parties were making their preparations.

Finally, the party would withdraw from *Philadelphia*, and escape on *Intrepid*. If the wind were favorable, they could sail out. Otherwise they could use sweeps – long oars intended to be used from the deck of a small ship – to row out of harbor. If all else failed, they could take to *Intrepid*'s boats, and row out to the waiting *Syren*, which would close on the coast once it saw the glow of the fires on *Philadelphia*.

To ensure that all went smoothly, Decatur broke the crew of *Intrepid* into six parties. One group – led by Jonathan Thorn – was to sail *Intrepid*, and would remain aboard the ship during the raid. This would mean that *Intrepid* was always available to support the withdrawal, and prevent it from drifting off during the raid. A second party would man *Intrepid*'s boats. Their mission was to provide security during the raid. They were to prevent any of *Philadelphia*'s Tripolitan crew escaping either by boat or by swimming, to take word of the raid to shore. They were also to provide a warning if boats from the harbor approached *Philadelphia* during the raid.

Four groups would board *Philadelphia*. These would be used to capture the frigate. Once the spar deck was under the control of the raiders, one group of men, led by Decatur, would remain on deck to provide security and to position the 18-pdr cannon. Three other groups – the incendiary parties – would retrieve parcels of combustibles from *Intrepid*, and use them to set fire to *Philadelphia*. A party led by Lieutenant James Lawrence would go to the frigate's forward berth and set fires

James Lawrence was an acting lieutenant on *Enterprise,* and led the incendiary party assigned forward. This painting shows him as a master-commandant in 1812. (USNH&HC)

US NAVY BOARDERS

The officers, sailors, and marines who participated in the raid must have felt as if they were taking part in a play. Instead of wearing their uniforms, they dressed as Mediterranean sailors. Stephen Decatur (center), one of the visible crew of *Intrepid*, dressed as a Maltese mariner, most likely as a ship's officer. In addition to his sword, like the rest of the officers in the party he carried a pair of Sea Service pistols. The weapons would have been hidden under his coat during the approach.

The two American sailors with him are dressed as a Sardinian (right) and an Arab sailor (left). These men were armed with either a cutlass or a boarding axe – cold steel was the order of the day. These men would also have doubled as members of the incendiary parties, once the ship was captured. This equipment would have included: (a) battle lanterns (carried by two or three men in each party); (b) incendiary material such as portfires, spermaceti candles, slow match, and gunpowder and turpentine sewn into canvas rolls (in the ditty bag); (c) loop of tarred canvas; (d) boxes filled with kindling (such as deal, wood shavings, and lint); and (e) buckets filled with tar.

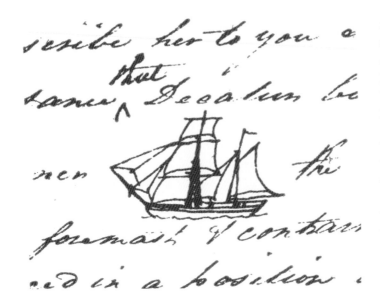

The only contemporary images of the short-lived *Intrepid* are midshipmen's sketches, like this one. (USNH&C)

in the forward storerooms. Bosuns' stores and the sail locker were both located near the bow, giving them plenty of inflammable material to work with. A second incendiary party, led by Lieutenant Joseph Bainbridge, would descend into the wardroom and steerage aft, and set their fires there. Finally, a group commanded by Midshipman Charles Morris would set fires in the cockpit and after storerooms in the midsection of the frigate.

This was all to be done at night, as quickly as possible, and with little margin for error. Decatur's raiders therefore drilled their tasks before departing from Syracuse, using *Constitution*. Although it was a larger vessel, *Constitution* was laid out in a similar manner to *Philadelphia*. The larger size worked to the advantage of the drilling raiders. When they carried out the raid in earnest, they knew they could reach their destinations and return to the spar deck in less time than it took during their practice sessions.

The order Preble finally issued to Decatur stated:

> It is my order that you proceed to Tripoli in company with the *Syren*, Lieutenant Stewart, enter that harbor in the night, board the *Philadelphia*, burn her and make good your retreat with the *Intrepid*, if possible, unless you can make her the means of destroying the enemy's vessels in the harbor, by converting her into a fire-ship for that purpose, and retreating in your boats and those of the *Syren*. You must take fixed ammunition and apparatus for the frigate's eighteen-pounders, and if you can, without risking too much, you may endeavor to make them the instruments of destruction to the shipping and Bashaw's castle. You will provide all the necessary combustibles for burning and destroying ships. The destruction of the *Philadelphia* is an object of great importance and I rely with confidence on your intrepidity and enterprise to effect it. Lieutenant Stewart will support you with the boats of the *Syren* and cover your retreat with that vessel. Be sure and set fire in the gun-room berths, cockpit, storerooms forward and berths on the berth deck. After the ship is well on fire, point two of the eighteen pounders, shotted, down the main hatch and blow her bottom out.

With orders in hand and the understanding that *Philadelphia* was to be burned and not recaptured, Decatur and Stewart sailed *Intrepid* and *Syren* from Palermo harbor on February 3 at 5:00pm. The plans were complete, the stores loaded, the men trained, and the officers eager. To maintain secrecy, *Syren*'s crew had not been informed of their destination or the actual mission until both ships were at sea. There would be no stops between Sicily and Tripoli. The next landfall would be Tripoli.

Preble's Boys

While Commodore Edwin Preble commanded the Mediterranean Squadron during 1803–04, he led a stellar collection of officers. Except for Oliver Perry, every naval officer serving in this squadron went on to command a US Navy squadron during a victorious naval battle or a single-ship duel in the War of 1812. Their future performance was often linked to Preble's skills as someone who fostered naval talent, and they were identified as "Preble's Boys." In the 1950s Fletcher Pratt wrote a book titled *Preble's Boys: Commodore Preble and the Birth of American Sea Power*. It named 15 officers as those whose careers benefited from Preble's tutelage. This claim, however, both overstates Preble's influence and is a bit unfair to "Preble's Boys."

Of Pratt's 15 officers, William Bainbridge was already a captain and only a little junior to Edwin Preble in 1803. *Philadelphia* was the fourth ship Bainbridge commanded (and the third and final one he would be forced to surrender to an enemy). Had Preble become indisposed before *Philadelphia*'s capture, Bainbridge would have taken over command. Today, we might possibly now be writing about Bainbridge's Boys. Four other members on Pratt's list – Lieutenants Jacob Jones and David Porter, and Midshipmen James Biddle and Daniel Todd Patterson – were aboard *Philadelphia* serving under Bainbridge. Preble's squadron arrived in May, and *Philadelphia*'s officers were imprisoned through the rest of Preble's tenure. They were not released until 1805. It is hard to see how Preble's leadership skills influenced their careers.

The remaining ten officers – Stephen Decatur, Isaac Hull, James Lawrence, Isaac Chauncey, William Burrows, Johnston Blakely, Lewis Warrington, Charles Stewart, Thomas Macdonough, and Stephen Cassin – had long and distinguished careers in the US Navy. Yet several of the young then-lieutenants who became the victorious captains of the War of 1812 – including Stephen Decatur, Isaac Hull, and Charles Stewart – were already marked as leaders before joining Preble. Along with Richard Somers, John Smith, and John Dent, Decatur, Hull, and Stewart were lieutenants commanding sloops and schooners in the 1803 Mediterranean Squadron. Others, most notably James Lawrence and Thomas Macdonough, were destined for leadership roles and set on the path to command because the captains of the ships in which they were serving recognized their abilities. Decatur, Hull, Lawrence, and Macdonough – along with David Porter of *Philadelphia* – had distinguished themselves by their performance in the Mediterranean in 1802–03, while Valentine Morris was commanding the American squadron in the Mediterranean.

Despite Preble's real leadership abilities, most of Preble's officers actually sank into obscurity. Shortly after Decatur's raid to burn the *Philadelphia*, Preble's squadron contained a total of 64 lieutenants, midshipmen, sailing masters, and master's mates – the pool from which future commanders would be drawn and which contained the ten cited as Preble's Boys. Several, including Charles Somers and Stephen Decatur's brother James, exited history's stage before delivering on their early promise – they were killed in combat during the Barbary Wars. Many others like Smith, Dent, and Joseph Bainbridge

Captain Edward Preble.
(USNH&HC)

(William's younger brother), led unspectacular yet competent careers. They lacked the spark of brilliance or dash of luck necessary to woo fortune.

That one-sixth of Preble's pool yielded future leaders speaks more of Preble's ability to discern leadership than to infuse it. Indeed, a better argument could be made that Preble's real strength was his ability to create an environment that gave talented officers the opportunities to excel. Unlike the indolent Morris, Preble kept his ships at sea, and aggressively sought the enemy. Preble dispersed his squadron in an effort to maximize the reach of the US Navy. Many other equally aggressive squadron commodores (including, ironically, Stephen Decatur when Decatur commanded a Mediterranean Squadron in 1815–16) kept the ships under their command together, treating individual warships as extensions of the commodore. Doing this expanded the commodore's control, but reduced the opportunities for individual initiative on the part of junior officers.

Preble's aggressiveness, combined with the degree of initiative and independence he gave even junior officers to pursue the enemy, provided a perfect context in which an outstanding leader could shine. Preble also encouraged his officers's inputs on how to strike the enemy. Decatur's attack on *Philadelphia*, for example, originated with a plan offered by Decatur himself. This willingness to allow junior officers the scope and opportunity to demonstrate initiative and competence was the real secret to Preble's ability to develop leadership.

**FEBRUARY 3
1804**

**5:00pm
Decatur and
Stewart sail
Intrepid and *Syren*
from Palermo
harbor**

THE RAID

Intrepid and *Syren* made a quick passage to Tripoli, reaching the Libyan coast on the afternoon of February 7. No one on shore realized that the two ships that appeared off the coast were anything other than two more merchantmen, carrying cargoes to the Moorish port. *Syren* had disguised its appearance and *Intrepid* was a merchantman.

Disguising *Syren* would have been simple. By striking the topgallant and royal masts and sails, and setting only one jib, Stewart would have made it appear less martial. Merchant vessels – with smaller crews than warships – sailed using more modest spreads of canvas than warships. Substituting smaller sails – using storm canvas rather than fair weather sails or setting foremast sails on the mainmast – would contribute to the illusion.

Simply handing the sails more slowly – taking in or shaking out a reef one sail at a time rather than trimming every sail simultaneously – would also cause observers to mistake *Syren* for a merchant ship. Warships prided themselves on smart sail handling, while merchant ship masters were more focused on economizing. Regardless which combination of techniques Stewart used to fool the enemy, he succeeded. Their arrival, perfectly timed to enter harbor under cover of dusk, seemed auspicious, and the two ships prepared to launch their planned attack.

No one was more eager to start the raid than the men aboard *Intrepid*. The ketch was packed with men, and most had to remain hidden below deck in the vessel's airless hold. Rotating the men allowed on deck did little to ease the crowding for those below. The little craft had other problems. The victualer responsible for supplying Preble's squadron had sent improperly

The fortifications and skyline of Tripoli as they would appear from a ship approaching the port. This was drawn by an officer in Preble's squadron. (LOC)

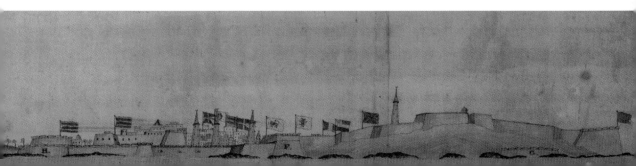

packed beef to Sicily. Some casks in which the salt beef had been stored had previously been used to store fish. These casks also leaked, allowing the pickle to seep out. The combination of previous use and inadequate pickle caused the beef in those casks to putrefy, and unfortunately the beef sent to *Intrepid* had come from this shipment. This fact went undiscovered until the ship was at sea, and the casks were opened. Then it was too late to turn back, too late to do anything other than dump the spoiled meat overboard. Other food aboard *Intrepid* was edible, but *Intrepid* was consequently short of supplies. The need for secrecy precluded a stop at Malta to replace the spoiled provisions. Decatur was forced to substitute extra bread in the men's rations for the missing beef, and hope they could complete their mission quickly. Decatur, Stewart, and the men aboard both American vessels soon had those hopes frustrated.

The Storm

As the ships began their approach to the harbor, the wind began picking up. Decatur already had a boat in the water to scout ahead. Waves were breaking over the rocks fringing the approaches, making entry impossible. Soon, a gale was blowing. The raiders found themselves caught in a violent squall, common off the African coast during the winter months. The scout boat returned to *Intrepid*, which was able to recover its crew, but the seas were so high that the boat had to be abandoned. The storm grew worse, pushing the two ships to the southeast, far out into the Gulf of Sidra. For the next eight days, *Intrepid* and *Syren* were forced to lie to, waiting for the storm to pass.

Conditions aboard *Intrepid* during the storm were miserable. Midshipman Charles Morris described them in his autobiography:

Charles Morris was the only early American naval officer to write an autobiography. It contains one of the most detailed accounts of the *Philadelphia* raid. Morris participated as a midshipman. (USNA)

The commander, three lieutenants, and the surgeon occupied the very small cabin. Six midshipmen and the pilot had a platform laid on the water casks, whose surface they covered when they lay down for sleep, and at so small a distance below the deck that their heads would reach it when seated on the platform. The marines had corresponding accommodations on the opposite side, and the sailors had only the surface of the casks in the hold. To these inconveniences were added the want of any room on the deck for exercise and the attacks of innumerable vermin which our predecessors the slaves had left behind them.

The only exercise afforded to the crew was the tedious and laborious task of manning the pumps – a labor needed frequently during the seven-day gale, as *Intrepid* leaked atrociously. To this situation was added the misery of a lack of food. Unsure how long the tempest would last and already low on food due to the bad beef, Decatur put the crew on short rations. For more than a week, the men aboard *Intrepid* lived mainly upon scanty portions of bread and water.

The storm finally eased on February 15. Heerman recorded that by that time the men aboard *Intrepid* were dispirited. Many felt that their prolonged presence off the coast must have roused the suspicions of those on shore. Some wanted to abandon the effort. Decatur – showing the qualities of personal example and magnetism that made him as great a leader as he was a fighter – roused the men's spirits by speaking with them. He restored their belief in the success of the attack.

As the weather eased, Decatur, Stewart, and their subordinate officers held a council of war aboard *Intrepid*. The two leaders agreed to return to Tripoli to try again. Stewart reinforced *Intrepid*, sending Decatur nine men under Midshipman Thomas Anderson in one of *Syren*'s boats. These reinforcements gave *Intrepid* a total of 84 men.

The two ships would sail independently, so as not be associated with each other, but would rendezvous at the entrance to the harbor after dark, at 10:00pm. Stewart planned to then transfer additional men from *Syren* to *Intrepid*, and final coordination between the two ships would then take place before the attack went in as planned.

Return and Approach

Intrepid and *Syren* returned to Tripoli the next day. The weather was fine, with a light wind, fair for the harbor. The weather was almost too good. The ships made so much progress that it looked as if they would arrive well before sunset. Waiting outside harbor until dark – or taking in sail to slow the ships – to ensure an evening arrival would have appeared suspicious. No legitimate merchantman would fail to take advantage of fair winds to make a daylight entry.

To slow the ships without making the ship appear to dawdle, sea anchors made from canvas and spare spars were set out, pulled behind the ship on a cable. These drags reduced the ships' speed without reducing sail, but would be invisible to an observer on shore. This was critical, as by now both ships could be seen from shore. Some of the American captives in Tripoli, prisoners from *Philadelphia*, saw the two ships approaching. They later wrote that they believed the ships to be American. Arab observers were apparently less discriminating, as the two ships failed to arouse their suspicions.

Decatur, with *Intrepid*, was 2 miles from the eastern entrance of the harbor at 6:30pm. He was supposed to wait for *Syren*, but the wind began falling as dusk approached. Decatur's seaman's instinct warned that this onshore breeze would die as night fell. In his report, made after the battle, he stated he was concerned that the wind would fail completely. Decatur therefore took in *Intrepid*'s sea anchors, and sailed into harbor, without waiting for Stewart. When Steward reached the rendezvous point two hours later, at 8:30pm, he saw *Intrepid* in the harbor's entrance. The onshore breeze of daytime was dropping to its nighttime lull, leaving *Syren* virtually becalmed at the rendezvous point.

Charles Stewart, then a lieutenant, was the senior officer on the raid. This picture shows him as a captain, c. 1815. (AC)

Stewart put 30 men in boats, under the command of James Caldwell, his senior lieutenant. Caldwell was in *Syren*'s launch containing 20 men. Sailing master Samuel Brook and nine others were in the ship's barge. Stewart ordered Caldwell to row to *Intrepid* and meet the ketch at Eastern Rocks, a landmark at the port's entrance. When he met *Intrepid*, Caldwell was to put his men under Decatur's command.

Caldwell never reached *Intrepid*. He signaled the ship with a lantern, but Decatur did not respond. Decatur was determined to reach *Philadelphia* while there was still wind to move his ship. Stopping for Caldwell's boats would take time. Moreover, stopping for boats from a second and apparently unrelated ship would appear unusual to onlookers. Bluff and the wind were the only two things that would get *Intrepid* to *Philadelphia*. The wind was dying, and any action that exposed the approaching ketch as more than an innocent merchantman would remove bluff from the table. Decatur therefore pressed deeper into the harbor. Caldwell's boats fell behind. Realizing that pursuit was hopeless and that all he could do was draw attention to *Intrepid*, Caldwell eventually stopped his chase, and waited by the Eastern Rocks to see how things developments.

Aboard *Intrepid*, final preparations had already been made. The combustibles, stored in tarpaulin-covered barrels, had been moved to

FEBRUARY 16 1804

6:30pm *Intrepid* arrives at rendezvous, two miles outside Tripoli harbor

Intrepid's deck. A final disposition of men was made. Decatur with two midshipmen and 14 sailors would hold *Philadelphia*'s upper deck, the spar deck. Lieutenant Thorn, Surgeon's Mate Heerman, and Pilot Catalano were given 13 men to handle *Intrepid* during its approach. These men were to remain with the ketch and defend *Intrepid* against any attack made from the harbor, while keeping the ship ready for departure when the raid was completed. Morris had eight men in his incendiary party. Lawrence was given Macdonough, Laws, and ten men. Bainbridge had Davis and ten sailors and marines. Finally, Anderson and his nine men from *Syren* were assigned to *Syren*'s boat. They were to watch the water around *Philadelphia*, and prevent members of the captured ship's crew from carrying the alarm to shore, whether in one of *Philadelphia*'s boats or by swimming. The frigate was moored less than 600 yards from shore – a long, but not impossible swim.

Most of the 84 men aboard *Intrepid* hid behind the bulwarks or crowded below deck where they could not be seen during the approach. Only a small party of sailors was visible on the decks, consistent with the crew of a merchant vessel. Among those on deck were Stephen Decatur and Salvatore Catalano. Like the rest of the men aboard *Intrepid* both those visible to observers and those concealed from sight, Decatur and Catalano were dressed like Maltese sailors. As *Intrepid* stood into harbor, it flew a British ensign Maltese ships would display, indicating they were protected by the crown – and Royal Navy – of Great Britain.

This disguise was all that stood between *Intrepid* and defeat. It took 2½ hours for *Intrepid* to cover the distance from the harbor's entrance to where *Philadelphia* was anchored. The ship was under the guns of both Tripoli's shore batteries and *Philadelphia* itself the entire time. To ward off any American attempt on the ship, the frigate's loaded guns were double-shotted (each gun was charged with two 18lb balls). Only a few hits on *Intrepid*'s light timbers with these guns would reduce the ship to a wreck.

No one aboard *Philadelphia* penetrated *Intrepid*'s masquerade as it ghosted towards the frigate on the dying evening breeze. Indeed, nobody even challenged *Intrepid* until nearly 9:30pm, when the ketch neared the prize. When *Intrepid* was just 100 yards from the frigate, someone on watch finally noticed it. He hailed *Intrepid*, ordering it to haul off. Catalano replied in Maltese. He shouted back to the frigate that his ketch had lost its anchors during the storm that had raged over the last week. He explained that the ship had been forced to stand offshore during the storm, unable to anchor, until the weather abated. He also asked permission to tie up to *Philadelphia* until morning.

It was a reasonable explanation for the ketch's behavior – anchors were easily lost during a storm. A ship dragging an anchors in a gale would have to cut its cable in order to stand into safer waters. Old anchors or those made from inferior iron frequently broke under the strain of a gale. Mediterranean anchors, such as those a tramp merchant vessel like *Mastico* would carry, were notorious for failing.

An anchorless ship in an unfamiliar harbor at night might easily prefer mooring to *Philadelphia* rather that trying its luck approaching a quay in

FEBRUARY 16
1804

8:30pm
Syren arrives
at rendezvous,
Intrepid is already
in the harbor

the darkness. The approach of the alien ketch – despite its Mediterranean and civilian appearance – had alarmed *Philadelphia*'s crew enough that they had removed the tampions from *Philadelphia*'s cannons, putting them at readiness to fire. Catalano's response soothed the suspicions of those aboard the frigate, however, and he was given permission to approach and tie up.

Catalano was questioned about the brig seen waiting offshore. This was *Syren*, but Catalano stated that it was *Transfer*, a brig recently purchased by Tripoli in Malta, which was expected to arrive shortly. Its captain, Catalano explained, had been unwilling to enter the harbor at dusk, and was waiting until morning before coming in. Another reasonable explanation, it further lulled suspicion. Catalano kept up a voluble conversation as *Intrepid* neared, further deflecting attention from other members of *Intrepid*'s crew.

Just as *Intrepid* reached *Philadelphia*, the wind shifted, then died completely. It last puffs pushed *Intrepid* away from the frigate, leaving the ketch 20 yards from its target. Decatur instructed Catalano to ask for a line from *Philadelphia*, so that *Intrepid* could pull itself to the frigate. Catalano relayed the request.

Intrepid sailing into Tripoli harbor as it approached *Philadelphia*. The wind was dropping and would die entirely before the ketch reached the frigate. (USNH&HC)

It was a measure of how thoroughly those aboard *Philadelphia* had been deceived that they not only agreed to pass a line to the strange ketch, but that they agreed to pull the ketch to the frigate. The officer in charge of the watch aboard *Philadelphia* called out a party of the men aboard his ship to assist the ketch, but insisted the Maltese craft send a boat to receive the line. The request allowed Decatur to execute an important part of his plan – to put Anderson and his party into *Syren*'s boat – without raising an alarm. The boat was being towed astern of *Intrepid*. With a measured sloppiness, the ten slipped into the boat, deliberately mimicking the behavior of a civilian crew. Anderson's men rowed the boat over to the frigate, took the offered line, and tied it to one from *Intrepid*, without generating suspicion on the part of the Tripolitans.

This activity consumed 30 minutes, during which period *Intrepid* lay under *Philadelphia*'s ready guns. Despite the tensions felt by the hidden raiders, none gave their presence away through premature action. As the American raiders waited, many of the men on watch aboard *Philadelphia* gathered on the forecastle, pulling the apparently harmless ketch closer.

Then, suddenly, just as *Intrepid* was about to reach *Philadelphia*, someone aboard the frigate realized something was wrong. Perhaps he realized that the ketch had more men aboard than was normal for a merchant vessel. Perhaps he finally recognized that the approaching vessel was the *Mastico*, a ship from Tripoli, and realized that since it had not announced its true identity, it must in American hands. For whatever reason, the man raised the alarm, shouting "Americanos." Other Arabs aboard *Philadelphia* soon echoed the cry.

Boarding and the Fight for the Deck

The warning came too late. Catalano urged Decatur to give the order to board, but Decatur felt the moment was not yet right. The distance between the ships was too wide to jump. *Intrepid* was still a few feet from *Philadelphia*, but momentum was carrying it towards the frigate. Decatur told his crew – now up from crouching behind the bulkheads and pouring up from below deck – to wait for his command. They did, poised on *Intrepid*'s bulwarks. As the ships touched, Decatur shouted "Board!"

Decatur intended to be the first American aboard *Philadelphia*, but lost his footing as he leapt, falling against the side of *Philadelphia*. He might have fallen into the sea between the two ships, but grabbed onto a chain plate – one of the steel bars used to guy the mast's shrouds – and hauled himself onto the deck. Decatur had been accompanied by two midshipmen – Charles Morris, commanding one of the incendiary teams, and Alexander Laws, part of James Lawrence's team. Laws clambered through one of *Philadelphia*'s gunports, snagging one of the pistols hung from his boarding belt as he wriggled through, delaying his entry. Morris, agile and powerfully athletic, leapt from *Intrepid*'s bulwark to *Philadelphia*'s forecastle, gaining the distinction of being the first American aboard the captured frigate.

His reward was almost to get skewered by Stephen Decatur. As Morris began down the spar deck in search of the enemy, a figure loomed out of the darkness, swinging a sword at him. It was Decatur, who had finally gained

TAKING THE *PHILADELPHIA*

FEBRUARY 16, 1804

Decatur's plan depended upon deception and surprise for success. It would only take a few hits from *Philadelphia's* 18-pdr long guns on the thin sides of the ketch to have sent *Intrepid* to the sea bottom. Decatur had to convince the Tripolitans that his ship was just a merchant vessel from Malta in order to get near enough to the frigate to board it. To foster that image, Decatur made careful preparations. He hid most of the boarding party below deck, keeping only enough men visible to be consistent with the small size of a merchant vessel. He also ensured everyone on the deck was dressed like a Maltese sailor and only allowed Salvatore Catalano – who spoke Maltese and Arabic in addition to his native Italian – to speak to those aboard *Philadelphia*. Decatur's deception was aided by his timing. The approach began at sunset, allowing him to enter the harbor under the cover of darkness. He also chose a quiet night, which lulled those aboard *Philadelphia* as well as those manning the shore batteries and other warships in the harbor.

US VESSELS

1 *Intrepid* towing *Syren's* boat

2 *Philadelphia*

TRIPOLITAN FORCES

1 Two xebecs, within 600 yards of *Philadelphia*

2 Brig-of-war

3 Gunboats

4 Bashaw's castle

5 Arsenal

6 Maltese castle

7 Mandrach castle

A late 19th-century painting of the boarding of *Philadelphia*. The most egregious error is not that the American sailors – who were disguised as Maltese and Arabs – are in uniform. It is that the uniforms are anachronistic, of a type worn only after the Civil War. (USNH&HC)

the deck and was seeking the enemy. Both men were dressed as "Arabs" – wearing clothing of Mediterranean sailors. Decatur, believing he was the only American aboard *Philadelphia* had assumed Morris to be part of the enemy's crew.

As previously noted, American sailors were given the password "Philadelphia" with which to identify themselves. Morris parried Decatur's blow, while bawling out "Philadelphia! Philadelphia!" Realizing his error, Decatur ceased attacking Morris and left, seeking legitimate prey.

Morris, Laws, and Decatur may have been the first three men from *Intrepid* to board, but they were quickly joined by all but the 14 men detailed to remain with Lieutenant Thorn, guarding *Intrepid*. Surgeon's Mate Heerman recorded that American sailors climbed over the side of the frigate like a swarm of bees. As with bees, the boarding party had a sting in the form of cold steel – cutlasses and boarding axes for the men and swords for the officers. The midshipmen, officially armed with dirks, almost certainly discarded these for cutlasses. Those that did keep them used their dirks as secondary weapons. The officers, midshipmen, and possibly the petty officers, also carried pistols. If these were used during this battle, their wielders applied them as clubs, rather than firearms. Considering the accuracy of Sea Service pistols, they were probably more effective when used that way.

Edged weapons proved sufficient for their task. During the entire fight to take *Philadelphia*, not one shot was fired by the Americans. The exact number of Tripolitan crew present aboard the frigate on the night of the raid is unknown. Possibly it was as few as 40 or as many as 150. Forty was probably too few given the ship's size and the number of guns in the frigate's battery, which was kept loaded. One hundred fifty was almost certainly too high given the subsequent ease with which the Americans retook *Philadelphia*. In all likelihood it was between 80 and 100 men.

Regardless of actual numbers, the Americans were prepared for combat, and the Tripolitans were not expecting a fight – certainly not hand-to-hand fighting aboard a ship anchored less than 600 yards from the Bashaw's castle. As the 70 armed Americans that boarded *Philadelphia* swept down the spar deck, the men they encountered were scattered, armed primarily with their personal knives or weapons improvised from what they found on deck – belaying pins, rammers, or handspikes. These defenders faced opponents armed with cutlasses, tomahawks, and club pistols, working together to overcome resistance. Because the Americans were dressed like them, the crew aboard *Philadelphia* could not know whether an approaching man was an ally or an enemy. The Americans were not similarly handicapped. Anyone bellowing "Philadelphia" was a friend who would guard your rear. Everyone else could be cut down with impunity.

In little more than the length of time it takes a healthy adult to jog 130ft, the Americans had cleared all Tripolitan sailors from *Philadelphia*'s spar deck. The biggest obstacle they faced there was the ship itself. Ducking under spars resting on the bulwarks and around the upper masts laid out on the deck probably slowed the progress of the American boarders more than any resistance from *Philadelphia*'s Arab crew.

Once the Americans cleared the spar deck, they descended the ladders to the main deck, where *Philadelphia*'s long 18-pdr cannon were mounted. There they again swept a deck clear of defenders. Although the men on the main deck had more time to prepare, the result was the same. After a brief struggle, the Americans owned the main deck as well as the spar deck.

It took only ten minutes to recapture *Philadelphia*. The American tars and marines killed 20 men of the frigate's crew and took one badly wounded man prisoner during the brief melee. The rest of the crew jumped overboard to swim for shore or ran to the illusionary safety of the frigate's hold. The boarders had suffered only one casualty – one sailor was slightly wounded.

OVERLEAF: The raiding party hid its true identity until it was too late for the Tripolitans. The American sailors climbed aboard the ship "like a swarm of bees," according to surgeon's mate Lewis Heerman. Armed only with edged weapons, the party won a rapid victory while incurring almost no casualties. The Americans were expecting trouble, but the Tripolitan crew was unready for combat. It was unarmed – weapons were not normally carried as part of shipboard routine – so they only had improvised weaponry: rammers, belaying pins, handspikes, and personal knives. The Americans, dressed like the Tripolitans, had an identifying watchword to differentiate friend from foe in the darkness. Individual, poorly armed Tripolitan sailors therefore had to face organized teams of Americans. *Philadelphia*'s crew either died – if they stood and fought – or fled. Lucky ones reached the bulwarks, jumped into the sea, and were able to swim to shore.

Lewis Heerman served as *Enterprise*'s surgeon, and accompanied Decatur in *Intrepid*. This image shows him as a senior navy surgeon in the 1840s. (FDRL)

As the fight for the deck raged, Anderson and his boat's crew attacked and captured the ship's boat that had been lowered from *Philadelphia* to pass the line to *Intrepid*. The battle in the boats was a miniature version of the battle aboard *Philadelphia*. The Americans – ready for battle – overwhelmed their opponents. The men in the boat were either killed by the Americans or jumped overboard to swim for shore. Heerman reported that Anderson interdicted the Tripolitans swimming for the shoreline, but there were too many for one boat to catch. Several escaped, to carry news of the American attack.

The Incendiary Parties

A brief lull followed the capture of *Philadelphia*. Ashore, in Tripoli, awareness grew that something was happening in the harbor. A pre-industrial city – lacking motor vehicles, powered machinery, and electricity

– was a quieter place than today's modern urban zone, especially after sunset. The clash of steel on steel, the shouting voices, even the splash of men jumping into the water would have been heard along the waterfront. It would have attracted attention, even if the cause of the noise was not yet understood.

At 10:00pm, when the attack started, most people would have been asleep. It took time for individuals to rouse themselves fully awake and comprehend what the noise meant. Some may have realized that an attempt on *Philadelphia* was being made. More minutes would have been spent deciding to act or – in the case of the naval and military leaders of Tripoli – to decide whether to turn their men out for action.

The pause gave Decatur time to take stock of the situation. He had the frigate in his possession. For the time being, Tripoli was quiet. There was nothing between *Philadelphia* and the Mediterranean Sea but a few miles of water. Decatur must have felt the tug of temptation, the urge to carry the frigate out to sea, and restore it to the US Navy.

Yet while Decatur always hungered for glory, he always tempered that hunger with reason. A brief glance at the ship showed that the only way it could leave harbor was under tow. The spars were down and were bare of canvas. Rousing the sails out of the sail lockers in the berth deck, and then bending the sails on with the 70 men Decatur had aboard the frigate, would take hours. Even if a tow line could be rigged from *Intrepid*, the ketch was significantly smaller than *Philadelphia*. Towing the frigate with *Intrepid* would like hitching a donkey to an ox cart.

The wind had also died. That meant *Intrepid* would have to use sweeps to move *Intrepid*, making a tow still more difficult. (Like most small sailing vessels, *Intrepid* was equipped with sweeps. These long oars could be fitted to small ports on the side of a ship along the main deck, so the ship could be moved by rowing. While at a pinch, a single man could operate a sweep, they were intended for use by multiple rowers, with two to four standing men on each sweep, walking as they pushed the shaft before them.) Preble's orders to burn *Philadelphia* and not attempt to cut it out of harbor, however pre-emptive they may have seemed to Decatur in Syracuse, now looked prescient. With what had to be great reluctance, Decatur gave the orders to burn the frigate.

The 34 men of the three incendiary parties made their preparations. Some of the men from each party returned to *Intrepid* to fetch combustibles, stored in barrels in the ketch. Soon they were passing packets of incendiary materials across to their mates on *Philadelphia*. These consisted of spermaceti whale-oil candles, gunpowder cartridges, turpentine-soaked canvas and lint, and small kegs and boxes filled with tar or wood shavings. Each party had several men who carried lit battle lanterns, from which the candles would be lit and used to ignite the rest of the material.

In a few minutes the materials were aboard *Philadelphia* and were distributed among the sailors in each team. Then, each group of men set off for their objectives. Lieutenant Lawrence's party was probably the first to reach its destination, since his goal was the forward berth deck and

**FEBRUARY 16
1804**

**10:00pm
Decatur orders
the boarding of
*Philadelphia***

storerooms. His men had the shortest distance to travel. *Intrepid* had come alongside *Philadelphia* towards the frigate's bow. Lawrence and his men would have descended to their objective via the fore companionway, a broad, ladder-like stair aft of the foremast. Additionally, one of the midshipmen assigned to Lawrence was Macdonough, who as noted was familiar with every detail of his old home.

Lawrence and his party – with Macdonough serving as guide – would have descended from the spar deck, past the gun deck into the berth deck, where the ordinary seamen in *Philadelphia*'s crew slung their hammocks. Some of Lawrence's men spread out across this space, collecting inflammable material – such as hammocks – to feed the fires their incendiaries would start. Others descended one level deeper, into the forward orlop platforms where the forward storerooms were located. These included rooms in which the boatswain's stores of cordage, tar, and turpentine were kept, the sailmaker's stores (filled with spare canvas), the gunner's storeroom, and the paint locker. All of these offered an environment that would foster flame.

Using the illumination offered by their battle lanterns, the men spread their parcels of incendiaries throughout this area. Lighting their spermaceti candles from the flame of the lanterns, the sailors then ignited the scattered incendiaries from the candles. After a brief pause to ensure that the flames had caught and were spreading, they scampered up the fore companionway to escape the pursuing flames.

Boarding actions – as illustrated in this painting of Decatur fighting the Tripolitans – were hard and brutal. (USNH&HC)

Joseph Bainbridge meanwhile took his party to the after companionway – forward of the mizzenmast down to the gun deck. From there, to reach the wardroom and after storerooms, his men would have had to go forward to the after ladderway – just ahead of the capstan. This ladder took them down one level to the berth deck. The after third of the berth deck was where the frigate's officers lived and slept. Along the sides of the ship were the officer's cabins – separated by partitions of deal, lathe, and canvas – which burned with ease. Between the cabins was the wardroom, where the officers dined. It too, offered fuel for a fire, in the form of chairs, cabinets, bookcases, and tables.

One level below the berth deck – and also accessible from the after ladderway – were the after orlop platforms. As with the forward orlop, this space was filled with storerooms – the bread room, purser's stores, and slop room filled with spare clothing, and officer's stores. All contained material that would feed flame.

The magazine was also in this area. Despite his party's incendiary activities elsewhere, Bainbridge had to ensure his men avoided starting fires near the magazine. A flame reaching the gunpowder would have caused an explosion – a result not desired until the incendiary party was back aboard *Intrepid* and *Intrepid* was well away from *Philadelphia*. Bainbridge and his men scattered their combustibles well aft of the magazine, in the after end of the wardroom, and in the store rooms at the stern of the ship. From there, it would take time for the flames to spread to the magazine. They, too, ignited the combustibles from their spermaceti candles. With fuel to feed the flames, these rooms were soon ablaze, the cloth and furniture igniting the timbers of the hull. Bainbridge, Midshipman Davis, and the ten men in Bainbridge's party began a race up the two sets of ladders to escape the flames that they had set.

While sources are unclear whether Lawrence's party or Bainbridge's men set the first fires aboard *Philadelphia*, it is agreed that Morris and his men were late to the party. Morris, the first man to board *Philadelphia*, led the last team to get their materials from *Intrepid*. Possibly this was because Morris, at the vanguard of the charge to take *Philadelphia*'s decks, had the longest distance to travel to get back to *Intrepid*. It may have been because Morris, a midshipman and the most junior officer of the three men leading incendiary parties, had been forced by his seniors to wait until they were done. Whatever the cause, by the time that Morris led his party of eight men down the companionway to the cockpit and store rooms amidships, fires had already been set in the two ends of the ship.

To compound Morris's troubles, as he rushed to the companionway he once again encountered Decatur. Decatur thought Morris was an Arab, a member of *Philadelphia*'s crew that had hidden below deck and was now seeking to escape the fires being set there. Decatur again swung his sword at Morris, who hastily parried, and again shouted "Philadelphia." Realizing his mistake, Decatur ceased attacking, and allowed Morris to pass.

Morris pressed on, reaching the cockpit, and had his men set fires in the frigate's midshipmen's quarters and operating theater, and in the storerooms immediately around the cockpit. By the time these had been set, the berth

Thomas Macdonough was a midshipman assigned to *Philadelphia*, but was detached from the frigate when it was captured. Transferred to *Enterprise*, he joined the party sent to burn his old home. (USNH&HC)

deck aft, one level above the cockpit, was already blazing. Flames blocked the way to the after companionway. Morris led his men to escape by moving forward, to the fore companionway. This part of the ship was filled with smoke, but the ladder was free of flames. Morris and his men soon reached the relative safety of the deck.

While the three incendiary parties were descending into *Philadelphia*'s hull, Decatur was managing affairs on its deck. He posted some of the 16 men and midshipmen that he retained upon the deck as lookouts, with instructions to pass the word if anyone approached *Philadelphia*. This duty would have required no more than a half-dozen reliable men. Decatur probably kept one of the two midshipmen with him, to serve as runners. The remainder may have formed a reserve, to respond to any unforeseen crises. It is also possible that a midshipman was detailed with a party to fulfill Preble's instruction to point two of *Philadelphia*'s 18-pdr cannon down the main hatch to blow out the frigate's bottom. It would have taken eight to ten sturdy men to drag one of these long guns into position.

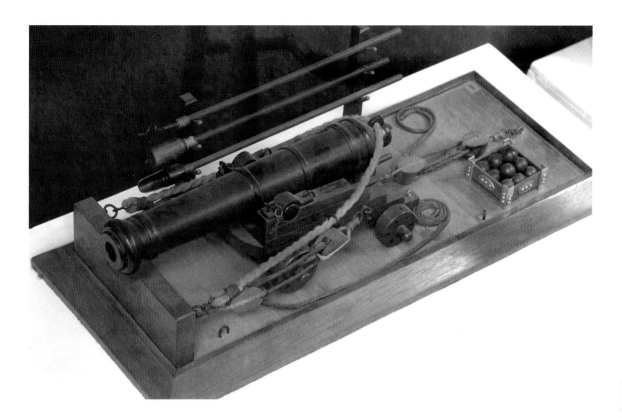

An 18-pdr long cannon. Decatur had instructions to use two of these guns to blow out *Philadelphia*'s bottom. The rapidity with which the fires grew made this impossible and unnecessary. (AC-HMM)

Whether the attempt was made to do this is unknown. In view of subsequent events, it is clear that even if a start had been made, the task was not completed. Decatur made no mention of moving the guns in his report of the action prepared for Preble after the raid. *Philadelphia*'s main battery guns were loaded and began firing as the ship burned. A gun fired down the main hatch would have punched a hole in the frigate's bottom, and the vessel would have sunk it where it was moored. This did not happen. Most likely, if an attempt to move two guns occurred, the sailors detailed to do this lacked time to complete their task. The incendiary parties worked quickly. They were back on deck within 15 minutes, and the fires they set spread swiftly. The men moving the cannon would have been forced to abandon the effort or perish in the flames – flames that made Preble's requirement superfluous.

By the time the last men of Morris's party regained the spar deck, the frigate was doomed. Anyone who remained aboard *Philadelphia* would join its fate, whether they be American raiders who delayed departure or any Tripolitan who had fled to the shelter of the frigate's hold when the Americans took the ship. Within 30 minutes of giving his order to board *Philadelphia*, Decatur ordered his men back to *Intrepid*. The final rush off the frigate was as precipitous as the rush to board the ship a bare half-hour earlier. A quick tally revealed that despite the rush, every man who had boarded *Philadelphia* was back aboard *Intrepid*, accompanied by a lone, wounded prisoner. The Americans had carried him with them rather than allow him to burn to death.

Tripolitan Reaction

It was as well that the Americans had done their work quickly. Even as Decatur directed his men off *Philadelphia*, Tripoli's defenders were reacting to the raid. The Tripolitan sailors from *Philadelphia* who had jumped into the water and been lucky enough to avoid Anderson while swimming away from the frigate were beginning to reach shore by this time. They alerted anyone who would listen that a raid was in progress. The fires aboard *Philadelphia* also served as an alarm. In a pre-industrial world, except for moonlight, nighttime darkness was absolute, even in cities. Any unusual light would be immediately noticeable.

On February 16, 1804, a thin crescent moon would have been low in the sky to the west at the time the raid started. The fires set in *Philadelphia* at first would have produced a glow of light around the ship, like electric lighting illuminating a modern ship today. Within 15 minutes of being set, flames could be seen at every gunport, hatch, and opening. As the fires grew, the light would have lit up the harbor.

Some of the city's defenders, however, were reacting even as the incendiary parties were beginning their destruction. Just before evacuating *Philadelphia*, lookouts reported that two Tripolitan xebecs just 200 yards from *Philadelphia* were preparing to move. As flames from the burning frigate illuminated the harbor, alarms were sounded throughout Tripoli. Shore batteries were being manned and gunboat crews making for their vessels. There was little immediate organized reaction, but the chaos on shore was steadily yielding to an ordered response.

Withdrawal

The immediate threat to the raiders as they fled *Philadelphia* was not the port's human defenders. Rather, it was the frigate they had come to destroy. Flames were billowing out of *Philadelphia*'s hold as the men aboard *Intrepid* cast off the lines mooring the ketch to the frigate. The Americans pushed off from *Philadelphia* with spars and shook out the ketch's furled sails. A line was passed down from *Intrepid*'s bow and lashed to Anderson's boat. Anderson turned *Intrepid*'s bow towards the harbor's exit to assist the departure. In the confusion, the boat launched by *Philadelphia* and captured by Anderson drifted away, unattended by its captors.

But the wind had died, and *Intrepid* hung motionless just yards from *Philadelphia*. Perversely, the wind then picked up and started sucking *Intrepid* back towards the frigate. Furnace-like heat rising from *Philadelphia*'s hatches ignited the tarred rigging that stayed the frigate's masts. Flames raced up the shrouds, turning the masts into towering, flaming beacons. The blaze generated a convection flow, with hot air rushing skyward, and heavier, cooler air flowing into *Philadelphia* from sea level. *Intrepid*, pulled by that draught, was being drawn to the flames. To add to the risk, the raiders had made an excess of combustibles. The incendiary parties had not been able to carry everything, and had left the surplus materials on *Intrepid*. These combustibles were on the deck, protected from burning sparks only by the barrel in which they were stored, and the tarpaulin that covered the barrel.

Decatur ordered the sweeps manned, and soon more than half of the men aboard *Intrepid* were pushing on the white-ash shafts of the sweeps, moving the ketch away from a fatal embrace with *Philadelphia*. *Intrepid*'s progress was aided by Midshipman Anderson and his men in *Syren*'s boat, who towed the ketch.

Progress was slow at first, but *Intrepid* steadily drew away from *Philadelphia*. Once *Intrepid* had moved far enough to escape the convection vortex, it caught a light wind. The offshore evening breeze was beginning, as heated air over the land's surface rushed to the cooler water. It was a fair wind for an escape from the harbor. The crew gave three cheers, exulting at both their success at burning the *Philadelphia*, and their escape.

Even as the threat of immolation faded, the frigate offered a fresh peril to *Intrepid*. Heat from the fire was igniting the charges in the frigate's guns. As the gunpowder "cooked off," the guns fired, discharging across the harbor the two iron shot loaded in each barrel. This gunfire was unaimed, but *Intrepid*'s path took it across *Philadelphia*'s field of fire. Cannonballs were soon whizzing around the ketch. Fortunately, none did any damage, and *Intrepid* was soon past the dangers posed by *Philadelphia*'s guns.

As one danger passed, another emerged. Even as *Intrepid* crawled away from *Philadelphia*, the defenders ashore, now fully aware that an American raiding party was in their harbor, were readying a response It came as *Intrepid*'s crew were completing their three cheers. Up until then, all of the fighting had been with edged weapons. Not a shot had been fired by either side. The echoing cheers appeared to serve as a signal. Every battery in the harbor fired its guns in the direction of the cheers, as if in response.

This salvo did no damage to *Intrepid* or its crew, but gunfire continued for a period of time. The shore batteries, unable to see anything clearly, except for the blazing *Philadelphia*, fired wildly into the harbor. The confusion was magnified when *Philadelphia*'s starboard battery – pointed towards shore – began randomly discharging. The waterfront was filled with buildings, and ships tied to quays and docks. Damage was scattered randomly, but every hit caused real destruction. It also generated the illusion that some force was guiding the fire from the frigate, dividing the attention of the port's defenders.

Soon, boats of every variety were setting into the harbor. Xebecs and other ships used for raiding slipped their moorings and took to the harbor's waters. They were joined by the gunboats intended to guard the harbor, and all manner of small craft and ships' boats. Many were filled with hastily assembled collections of Arab and Turkish sailors, heading for the sound of combat. Others were merely responding to the mariner's instinct – that trouble was better faced at sea than on land.

At the castle that formed the home and principal fortification of Yusuf Karamanli, the ruler had been roused by the commotion in the harbor. He mounted the fort's ramparts in time to see his prize blazing in the harbor. All he could do was watch impotently. The battle was beyond his control.

For the men aboard *Intrepid* one final task remained: escape. If taken prisoner, they would not have been killed. Captives were too valuable to kill

INTREPID'S ESCAPE

FEBRUARY 16, 1804

While Tripoli harbor was quiet during *Intrepid*'s approach, departure was livelier. As *Intrepid* sailed out of harbor, the night was illuminated by the burning *Philadelphia*, blazing like a torch. Additional illumination – and noise – was provided by the harbor's batteries, firing to intercept the unknown enemy. The harbor was also alive with ships and boats. Some of them were warships, seeking out the American raiders. Others were merchant vessels working towards the safety of the quays or the open sea, or any other refuge. The confusion aided *Intrepid*'s escape. *Intrepid*, smaller than *Philadelphia*, had tied up on the seaward side of the frigate, hidden from observers on shore by the bigger vessel. The raid started and finished in the remarkably short period of 30 minutes. The speed with which the Americans attacked meant that *Intrepid* was away from *Philadelphia* before most observers on shore were aware an attack was happening. No one in Tripoli knew what ship had attacked. The innocent-looking ketch was allowed to depart unmolested, with observers assuming it was just another merchant vessel seeking safety.

US VESSELS

1. *Intrepid* towing *Syren's* boat
2. *Philadelphia* burning

TRIPOLITAN FORCES

1. Bashaw's castle
2. Arsenal
3. Maltese castle
4. Mandrach castle

outright, either because of their ransom value or their price when sold as slaves. The *Intrepid* men would have been subject to both ill-treatment and beatings, however. This was the fate of the captive American crew of *Philadelphia* in the weeks following the raid. The officers housed in the castle were moved to cells and strictly confined after the frigate was burned. The enlisted members of its crew, housed in a verminous warehouse prior to the raid, found that the frequency of the beatings increased, the quantity and quality of the food decreased, and that their workload was multiplied in the wake of *Philadelphia*'s destruction. If *Intrepid*'s crew were captured, they would likely have fared far worse.

But the wind was fair for exit and the offshore breeze gained strength. *Intrepid* moved steadily, if slowly, through the waters of Tripoli harbor under all plain sail – topgallant, topsails, and courses. Anderson and his men followed in their boat. Most likely a line had been passed down to the cutter and it was being towed by *Intrepid*. It would have been a long pull for the crew of a ship's boat who had been involved in strenuous activity for over an hour, and there is no mention of *Intrepid* stopping to pick up the boat.

Intrepid experienced little trouble during its withdrawal. Of the hundreds of rounds fired by the harbor's batteries and ships during the confused hour following *Philadelphia*'s ignition, only one struck *Intrepid*. A ball flew though the main-topgallant sail, punching a small hole in the canvas.

Intrepid barely escaped the conflagration its crew had set. The draught of *Philadelphia*'s flames forced them to use sweeps to move away. (USNH&HC)

The damage was insignificant. As was common in naval combat, especially at night, the gunners were firing too high.

Furthermore, once *Intrepid* had left the immediate vicinity of *Philadelphia*, it would have been virtually undetectable as an American warship. The ship was originally from Tripoli, in rig and appearance typical of the scores of ships that sailed out of the port. The port was swarming with these types of vessels in the aftermath of the attack. Some of these were seeking out the intruders, but many other ships were simply attempting to get out of harm's way. As long as *Intrepid* did not draw undue attention to itself, it could pass as one of these craft.

In the darkness, and given the confusion that followed the raid, about the only thing that *Intrepid* could have done to have marked itself as an American ship would have been to have its crew start singing "Yankee Doodle." Other ships were firing guns, maneuvering wildly, or acting in a manner similar to *Intrepid* on its way out of the harbor. Only a relative handful of men aboard the Tripolitan ships were even aware that *Philadelphia* had been attacked by a ketch – an unlikely craft for such an operation. *Intrepid* had approached *Philadelphia* during dusk, and had tied up to the seaward side of the frigate. The frigate would have obscured the ketch from waterfront observers, even those on the two xebecs moored closest to *Philadelphia*. As long as the American members of the crew remained quiet and let pilot Catalano answer all challenges, detection was unlikely. So it proved. In his post-action report, Decatur noted, "Many boats filled with men lay round, but from whom we received no annoyance."

Behind them was the burning *Philadelphia*, unforgettably captured in the memories of those present. Morris described the scene in his memoirs:

> The appearance of the ship was indeed magnificent. The flames in the interior illuminated her ports and, ascending her rigging and masts, formed columns of fire, which, meeting the tops, were reflected into beautiful capitals; whilst the occasional discharge of her guns gave an idea of some directing spirit within her. The walls of the city and its batteries and the masts and rigging of cruisers at anchor, brilliantly illuminated and animated by the discharge of artillery, formed worthy adjuncts and an appropriate background to the picture.

Finally, perhaps an hour after *Intrepid* left *Philadelphia*, the ketch was approached by *Syren*'s launch and barge, occupied by James Caldwell and his party of 30 sailors from the brig. Having been left behind by Decatur at 9:00pm, they had waited near the Eastern Rocks, on what they assumed would be *Intrepid*'s escape route.

Decatur was surprised by their appearance. Initially he believed them to be boats from the harbor, finally attempting to block the departure of the ketch. But once he realized what they were, he welcomed the reinforcement. Thirty extra armed men in two additional boats gave Decatur a force that could contend with any combination of light boats, or any single gunboat or galley, that might attack the Americans as they left harbor. It would take one of the xebecs to bar an American departure, and they were not in evidence.

Philadelphia burning in Tripoli harbor. The fires were set within a 30-minute period. (USNH&HC)

**FEBRUARY 16
1804**

**10:30pm
Philadelphia is
fired, Decatur
orders the
withdrawal**

Intrepid met no serious opposition during the rest of her escape, but it took 90 more minutes for *Intrepid* and its escorting boats to reach *Syren*. Stewart, in his report, stated the rendezvous occurred at 1:00am. The arrival of the ketch was greeted with repeated cheers from *Syren*'s crew. At that point, any chance the Tripolitans had to capture the raiding force was gone. *Syren*, with its battery of 24-pdr carronades, could make short work of two lightly timbered xebecs. (Stewart had his ship cleared for action, and his men at the guns since 8:30pm the previous night.) The American ships were 5 miles from shore, and well out of range of shore batteries.

The cost to the Americans had been trivial. The *Intrepid*'s men had taken just one casualty – one man had been wounded by a blade during the struggle for *Philadelphia*'s deck, but the cut was minor. The only disappointment felt by the raiders at their rendezvous was a lack of trophies from the raid. They had taken the Tripolitan flag off *Philadelphia*'s flagstaff, intending to carry it away. Somehow, during the hurried departure from *Philadelphia*, it had been left behind. The boat that Anderson's cutter had captured drifted away during the confused departure. The prisoner they had taken would die of his wounds, despite Surgeon's Mate Heerman's best efforts to save him.

Stewart hoisted in *Syren*'s three boats, and recovered the crewmen whom he had loaned to Decatur. Stewart took *Intrepid* under tow, to speed their departure. He had the topgallant masts and spars restored, set sail and set a course north-northeast for Syracuse. At 4:00am, with *Syren* under easy sail, and *Intrepid* bobbing along after the brig, Stewart finally had *Syren*'s crew stand down from their action stations. He ordered the guns housed and shipped the gunports, ready for a run to Sicily.

Some of the Tripolitan artillery that Decatur had to face in his attempt to burn *Philadelphia*. These guns were later captured by the US Navy and are now on display in Washington DC. (Bruce Biskup photo)

**FEBRUARY 17
1804**

**1:00am
Intrepid
rendezvouses with
*Syren***

AFTERMATH

Philadelphia burned on long after the Americans departed. At 11:00pm the frigate's masts and tops collapsed, an event observed and logged by *Syren*, waiting outside the harbor. Finally, near midnight, the flames ate through the cables mooring the ship to its anchorage. The blazing vessel then began drifting, sluggishly moving with the tugging currents in the harbor. Eventually, the ship's keel grounded in shallow water near the castle, where Karamanli stood watching. Well after midnight, the flames finally ate down to the frigate's magazines. The subsequent explosion rocked the town, showering the vicinity with flaming debris thrown up by the blast, causing yet more damage to the waterfront.

But the explosion – as massive as it was – failed to extinguish the fires on the frigate. *Philadelphia* continued to burn until the flames consumed every combustible part of the ship above the waterline. Not until well after dawn had broken on the following morning did the fire burn itself out. Stewart reported seeing the glow from the burning frigate in the morning twilight, at 6:00am, when *Syren* and *Intrepid* were 40 miles from the port.

Only a few charred timbers remained of what previously had been one of the most powerful frigates in the world. Had Decatur been able to carry out his order to blow out the frigate's bottom with its own guns, the Tripolitan government could possibly have salvaged *Philadelphia*. The ship would have sunk in waters deep enough to cover the hull and extinguish the fires that had been set. Instead, fire destroyed the ship beyond any opportunity of repair.

Eventually, the rulers of Tripoli had slaves fill in the remaining timbers of the hull with rock – *Philadelphia*'s bones became the foundation of a new quay. It was a far cry from what they had hoped they could get out of the frigate when it first fell into their hands, but it was the only remaining use they could squeeze out of their prize.

The wind, which had been so calm during *Intrepid*'s approach to *Philadelphia*, gained strength during the ship's departure from the harbor as night yielded to day. By 9:00am a strong breeze was blowing, so stiff that

Syren shortened sail. But the wind was fair for Syracuse, and both ships were homeward bound.

The need to disguise *Syren*'s naval character was no longer required. Stewart restored the brig's warship's rig, setting up the royal masts, and putting out every stitch of sail *Syren* could carry, including topgallant and royal stay sails. Even towing *Intrepid*, the ship made a fast passage. The return trip to Syracuse was completed in just 36 hours. They arrived at Syracuse at 9:00am on February 19, 1804.

Constitution was anchored in port with Commodore Preble aboard. *Intrepid* and *Syren* were arriving more than a week later than they were expected to return. With their fast passage from the Gulf of Sidra, the ships had outrun the news of their exploit in Tripoli harbor. Preble had been awaiting word of the outcome of the raid in an agony of uncertainty over that period, his concern growing with every day the two ships failed to appear. As soon as the lookouts on *Constitution* reported the appearance of his missing ships, the Commodore signaled *Syren*, asking about the outcome of the attempt. *Syren* signaled the raid's success.

The wind was dying. Knowing that Preble wanted a full report immediately, Stewart, the senior officer, went to *Constitution* in one of *Syren*'s boats. *Syren* and *Intrepid* entered Syracuse under sweeps. When *Syren* and *Intrepid* passed the flagship, two hours later, Preble had ordered the yards and rigging manned to salute the ships. The frigate's crew gave three cheers, which were returned by *Syren* and *Intrepid*. *Vixen* and *Nautilus*, also in port, rendered similar honors as the two victorious raiders passed them. Their cheers were enthusiastically returned.

Decatur and Stewart had one last piece of business to attend to before they could write their reports and complete their participation in the raid to burn *Philadelphia*. The putrid beef carried by *Intrepid*, stores that had imperiled the success of the mission, was surveyed in accordance with the regulations of the US Navy and formally condemned as unfit for consumption.

Philadelphia adrift in Tripoli harbor after the fires burned through its mooring lines and its masts had fallen. (FDRL)

STEPHEN DECATUR

Born in 1779, Stephen Decatur was the best-known captain in the US Navy between its creation in 1798 and the end of the War of 1812. His family came from Philadelphia, but Decatur was born in Maryland's Eastern Shore – his mother fled Philadelphia after the British occupied that town in 1777. Decatur was born to the sea. His grandfather and father were mariners, and prior to the American Revolution, Decatur's father, Stephen Decatur Sr, captained merchant ships. During the Revolution, Decatur Sr served in the Continental Navy. He was later appointed captain in the US Navy after it formed in 1798.

Stephen Decatur secured a midshipman's warrant on April 30, 1798, aboard the *United States*. The ship was then commanded by his father's friend and Revolutionary War naval hero John Barry. *United States* was put in commission as part of America's naval mobilization during the Quasi-War with France. During that war, it patrolled in the Caribbean. During that period, Decatur established his reputation for courage and concern for the sailors. When a seaman fell overboard, Decatur jumped after the man, keeping him afloat until a boat was lowered to recover seaman and officer. Mr Midshipman Decatur was promoted to lieutenant on May 21, 1799, and was retained by the Navy after the Quasi-War. He was first sent to the Mediterranean in 1801–02 as part of the first US Navy squadron sent to deal with the Barbary States. On that cruise he served as first lieutenant of *Essex*, and then as the first lieutenant of the *New York* in the 1802–03 squadron. In 1803–04 he was named lieutenant-commanding of the schooner *Enterprise*. As such, he captured the Tripoli warship *Mastico*. The prize,

Stephen Decatur in 1805. (USNA)

renamed *Intrepid*, became the platform from which Decatur would launch his assault on *Philadelphia*.

The action in Tripoli harbor made Decatur's reputation. Horatio Nelson called it "the most bold and daring act of the age." It caught the imagination of the American public, and the gratitude of Congress. They promoted Decatur to captain, jumping him over more senior lieutenants in the US Navy. He was 25. After Commodore Edward Preble was superseded by Samuel Barron as commander of America's Mediterranean Squadron in September 1804, Decatur took command of the 44-gun frigate *Constitution*. He returned to the United States in 1805, following peace with Tripoli. On March 6, 1806, he married Susan Wheeler. While the marriage remained childless, the two remained deeply in love for the rest of Decatur's life. In 1807 the frigate *Chesapeake*, sailing to the Mediterranean, was stopped by the British warship *Leopard*, and forced to surrender three crewmen to the British. Its captain and the Mediterranean Squadron commander, Commodore James Barron, was relieved and Decatur took command of *Chesapeake*. With *Chesapeake*, and a flotilla of gunboats, Decatur patrolled the American coast to repel any further British attempts to interfere with American shipping. Decatur also sat on the court-martial board investigating the performance of the officers aboard *Chesapeake* during *Leopard*'s attack. The board suspended Barron from the US Navy as a result.

In 1810, Decatur took command of *United States*, one of three Humphreys frigates designed to carry a main battery of 24-pdr long guns. When the War of 1812 started,

United States was part of a squadron commanded by Commodore John Rodgers. The squadron was sent to intercept a homeward-bound Jamaica convoy. Rodgers' squadron failed to find the convoy, but encountered HMS *Belvadera*, which was pursued but ultimately escaped. The squadron broke up soon afterward, and *United States* continued independently.

Shortly afterwards, *United States* encountered HMS *Macedonian*. Two years earlier, when at peace, Decatur and John Carden, *Macedonian*'s captain, wagered their hats on which frigate would win if the two ships ever met. Decatur answered the question decisively, quickly reducing *Macedonian* to a hopeless state. After it became apparent that *Macedonian* was unmaneuverable, Carden surrendered. Decatur avoided damaging the British ship unnecessarily. He instead repaired it, and carried his prize into New London, the first major British warship taken as a prize by the American navy in that war. It renewed his fame among the American public.

The rest of the War of 1812 was frustrating for Decatur. He was blockaded in port by the British in New London, unable to take *United States* to sea. In August 1814, Decatur transferred to New York, where he took charge of the city's naval defenses and the frigate *President*. In January 1815, Decatur sailed from New York in *President*, but it grounded leaving harbor, damaging the vessel. Humiliatingly for Decatur, he was then out-thought by an opponent – for perhaps the first time in his career. John "Magnificent" Hays, commanding an opposing British squadron, anticipated where Decatur would go and intercepted *President*. Trapped by the squadron, a final escape attempt blocked by HMS *Endymion*, Decatur was forced to surrender. The war was near its conclusion, however, and Decatur was paroled and then released.

After the war's end, in late 1815, Decatur took command of one of two American squadrons sent to the Mediterranean again to put down the Barbary States. He hustled his squadron to the Mediterranean, as the second squadron was commanded by William Bainbridge, Decatur's superior due to seniority. Before Bainbridge could arrive, Decatur forced the surrender of several of the Barbary States, and was present at the capture of the Algerine frigate *Mashuda*. The surrenders proved temporary, but the arrival of Bainbridge's squadron, which included a ship-of-the-line, led to a permanent peace settlement and put an end to the depredations of the Barbary States.

Monument to Stephen Decatur. (AC)

After returning from the Mediterranean in 1816, Decatur was appointed to the Board of Naval Commissioners in Washington DC, the body that determined naval policy. In 1820, James Barron, restored to the US Navy after the War of 1812, challenged Decatur to a duel. Barron claimed that comments that Decatur made about his conduct during the 1807 *Chesapeake–Leopard* incident impugned Barron's honor. Oversensitive on matters of honor, Decatur accepted the challenge. Both officers were badly wounded during the duel, which took place on March 22, and Decatur soon died of his injury.

ANALYSIS

American success at Tripoli was not pre-ordained, despite the seeming ease with which it was accomplished. Close examination of the raid shows that the raid teetered on the edge of failure at many points. The storm on February 7 and the bad beef aboard *Intrepid* almost combined to abort the attempt before it could be launched. The second try, on February 16, had frequent crisis points where bad decisions could have pitched the attack into disaster. Four major factors led to American success. These were: Decatur's decision not to wait for *Syren*; the presence of Salvatore Catalano; Preble's order to burn *Philadelphia*; and the speed with which the actual attack was conducted.

Decatur's decision to press on without *Syren* has been cited as both an example of bold initiative and an attempt to demote Stewart from the raid's senior officer to a mere observer. Most participants agree that the original plan involved having both ships enter the harbor. The boats of the *Syren* were to support the attack and *Syren* was to "cover your retreat." It was difficult for Stewart and his crew to do either, with *Syren* outside harbor, and the ship's launch and barge resting on their oars at the Eastern Rocks. By sailing in unaided, Decatur *did* guarantee that any credit would go to him and the men aboard *Intrepid*.

As measured by results, the scales fall on the side of bold initiative, however. Decatur sought personal glory throughout his career, but never at the expense of failing in his mission. Although the plan called for him to wait, Decatur knew the wind was falling. He realized that *Syren*'s presence could improve his chance of success, but he also was a consummate mariner. He judged that the wind could die completely before he could reach *Philadelphia* if he waited.

As was seen in the description of the raid, the wind continued to fall throughout *Intrepid*'s approach. The wind at the harbor's entrance left *Syren* becalmed outside Tripoli when Stewart finally arrived. While there was still some breeze within the harbor at that time, the wind died completely with *Intrepid* 20 yards from its prey. Had Decatur rigidly adhered to the previous day's plan, both American ships would have been outside the harbor looking in from 8:30pm, when *Syren* arrived, until 11:00pm when the offshore breeze finally reached the harbor's entrance. Since that wind was blowing to the north, any approach would have been much longer than the three hours used by *Intrepid*.

The presence of Salvatore Catalano was a second major factor in the raid's success. Had the Sicilian pilot not participated in the attack, it is unlikely that *Intrepid* would have successfully deceived the Tripolitan crew of *Philadelphia*. The men aboard the frigate were anticipating some type of American effort to retake the ship. The frigate's guns were loaded. The ketch's approach even led the frigate's crew to remove the tampions covering the muzzles of its cannon, an action taken in preparation for combat.

Catalano single-handedly convinced *Philadelphia*'s crew that *Intrepid* was a harmless merchant vessel. He spoke Maltese fluently enough to satisfy his listeners that he came from that island. No American could have done that. He provided a plausible reason to approach *Philadelphia*, and his gossipy exchanges with the watch aboard the frigate further deflected suspicion. He even talked *Philadelphia*'s crew into helping *Intrepid* bridge the final 20 yards separating the two ships.

During its painfully slow approach, the ketch spent more than an hour sat less than 100 yards from the frigate, in the arc of fire of its broadside. If Catalano not been aboard or had he made a slip, *Intrepid* would most likely

A detail from an 1804 map showing Tripoli harbor, drawn by an officer aboard USS *Syren*. (LOC)

have been sunk before it reached *Philadelphia* – double-shotted 18-pdrs would have torn *Intrepid* apart with just a few hits. Indeed, had *Philadelphia*'s occupiers had even ten minutes' warning in which to arm and prepare themselves to repel boarders, the attempt to destroy the frigate would have been foiled. That they did not was due primarily to Salvatore Catalano.

Preble's decision to order *Philadelphia* burned rather than retaken was a major reason that the raid succeeded, although it may seem strange today. Even at the time, some – including Jacob Jones, one of *Philadelphia*'s lieutenants imprisoned in Tripoli when the raid occurred – questioned why Decatur did not attempt to retake the ship. Twenty years after the raid, Jones wrote: "I know of nothing which could have rendered it impracticable to the captors to have taken the *Philadelphia* out of the harbor of Tripoli." Yet, Preble's orders were prudent, given communications in 1804 and the nature of Stephen Decatur.

In 1804, news traveled at the speed of a sailing ship. When Preble issued his orders, he was more than 250 nautical miles from the frigate and the most recent information he had from Tripoli was weeks old, with only vague reports of the ship's condition. There must have been tremendous temptation for him to give the man at the scene latitude to make the final decision whether to destroy or retake the ship.

Yet Preble instead gave only one course of action. Depending on the wind, it could take an additional week for Decatur and Stewart to reach Tripoli. Much could have changed in a month, but it was highly unlikely that *Philadelphia* – even if a new foremast had been stepped – would be ready to sail. Before Decatur could attempt to take *Philadelphia* out of harbor, he would therefore have to spend valuable time checking to see if *Philadelphia* could sail – time that would allow a Tripolitan response to develop.

Even if *Philadelphia* had its sails on its spars, ready to be set, sailing it out of harbor would have been extremely risky. The raid was being mounted at night, in an unfamiliar harbor. *Philadelphia* was a deep draft ship, and Tripoli harbor had many shoals – such were what led to the frigate's capture in the first place.

Would Decatur have tried to take the ship out, regardless of these risks? Quite possibly, given his personality. Preble knew that. Destroying *Philadelphia* or restoring the frigate to the US Navy would restore the balance of power in favor of the United States and gain Decatur additional glory. Yet Preble knew that failure – leaving *Philadelphia* in Tripolitan hands after a botched recovery – would cost the United States more that it could benefit from the frigate's recapture. Better the certain destruction of the ship than its possible restoration, especially since the nature of the raid – with its dependence upon surprise for success – meant that the United States would only get one try.

Preble's decision simplified and focused the raid. A raid intended to destroy *or* sail the frigate out of harbor would have been much harder to mount. It would have required planning to carry out one of two mutually contradictory objectives. Cutting the frigate out of port required a completely different set of preparations and tools than burning the ship. Preble knew the raid would be led by junior officers – lieutenants in their early and mid twenties. Deciding whether to burn the frigate or sail it out of port – with limited time to weigh alternatives – required experience that junior officers lacked. Preble himself had the requisite experience, but his responsibilities dictated that he remain at Sicily, in command of the entire squadron. He judged it best to keep things simple. Recovering *Philadelphia* was a luxury. Denying it to Tripoli was the necessity. Recovered or destroyed it would be denied to Tripoli, but it was simpler to destroy the ship.

In hindsight we can see that conditions made it impossible to cut out *Philadelphia*. The sails were not on the spars when Decatur arrived. Even if they had been, the foremast had not been replaced and the mainmast lacked the stay that would have attached to the foremast. Only the mizzen was capable of carrying canvas without risking the loss of the mast. Finally, *Intrepid* arrived during a period of still air. Without wind, *Philadelphia* would be going nowhere. When the wind did return, it was light. It took *Intrepid* nearly two hours to sail out of the harbor. It escaped unmolested from the (by then) crowded harbor only because it appeared to be just another panicking merchant ship. Had Decatur and his men been sailing *Philadelphia*, they would have been noticed. The frigate would almost certainly have suffered attack by the ships in the harbor or the shore batteries during the two hours it would have needed to escape. Destruction or recapture would have been almost inevitable.

The American raiding party's capture of *Philadelphia* took no more than ten minutes, and the incendiary parties completed their work in less than 20. From the time someone aboard *Philadelphia* called out the warning "Americanos" until the last American sailor abandoned the then-burning frigate for *Intrepid*, only 30 minutes passed. The very speed of the attack was the final major factor in the raid's success, for several reasons. It is likely that the frigate's crew outnumbered the American attackers. The frigate's defenders were unable to use that advantage due to the speed with which the Americans boarded *Philadelphia* – it denied them time in which to organize a response. Individual Tripolitan sailors, pitted against groups of American sailors and marines, had little time to take up arms and were instead faced with three bad choices – stand and die, jump overboard and swim for shore, or take refuge in the ship's hold.

The speed with which the incendiary parties started their fires also prevented any effective outside response once the Americans gained control of the frigate. Many Tripolitan forces were close to *Philadelphia*. The frigate was moored less than 800 yards from shore, under the guns of the Bashaw's castle. There were two xebecs tied up only 400 yards from *Philadelphia*. The xebecs with their crews, armed and turned out at their stations, could have covered the distance between their quays and *Philadelphia* in about 12 minutes. Even under these optimal conditions, however, the Tripolitans would barely have had enough time from the initial cry of "Americanos" to reach *Philadelphia* before the incendiary parties began their descent inside the frigate.

Conditions on shore were far from optimal. Crews – of both ships and fortifications – were largely asleep when the raid started. Men were likely in barracks rather than aboard their ships or at the embrasures of their shore batteries. Even so, the shore response eventually came – the *Intrepid*'s cheers after clearing *Philadelphia* were greeted by massed artillery fire. The cheering occurred perhaps 45 minutes after the alarm was raised aboard *Philadelphia*, too slow a response to permit Tripoli to preserve their prize.

The speed with which the US Navy force conducted the attack was the result of careful planning, meticulous organization, and painstaking practice. Decatur had picked motivated, capable men, and divided his force into organized parties prior to leaving Sicily. Each member of the expedition was given an assignment and drilled in its responsibilities before entering Tripoli

harbor. Preble, Decatur, Stewart, and the leaders of each party thrashed out the scenario they planned, and ensured that each man had all the resources necessary to carry out his task. Combustibles were prepared before leaving, and the raid rehearsed aboard *Constitution*. Decatur's attention to detail even extended to such items as establishing a system of identifying friend from foe on a dark deck when both sides were dressed alike.

The result was an action that despite the very real difficulties involved was executed in a manner that made it seemingly effortless. The very speed of the attack meant that few of the harbor's defenders could identify the ship responsible, and allowed *Intrepid* to escape unmolested.

The account presented in this book differs from standard narratives on several points. Most accounts state that *Intrepid*'s crew pulled the ketch to the frigate after *Philadelphia* passed a line across. Several American accounts by participants relate the passing of the line to Anderson, yet they are less clear as to which craft provided the manpower to draw the ships closer together. A merchant ketch would have a crew of only about 20 men. Ten men were in the boat with Midshipman Anderson. Unless Decatur was willing to have more of the hidden men reveal themselves – which he would want to avoid, given the need to avoid rousing suspicion – too few men would have been left on *Intrepid* to allow its crew to pull the ships together.

A romanticized picture of Decatur fighting a Barbary captain in single combat. (AC)

69

Philadelphia had a warship's crew aboard, even if it was an abbreviated crew. It seems more likely that the officer of the watch gathered whatever spare hands were awake to have them attend to the job. This would also help explain why *Philadelphia* fell as quickly as it did. Using part of *Philadelphia*'s watch to pull *Intrepid* in would have clustered a significant percentage of the watch into an unarmed party vulnerable to an unexpected rush of boarders.

American participants also claimed that *Philadelphia*'s Tripolitan crew lowered a boat from the frigate as American boarders attacked the spar deck in an effort to escape. Anderson's men, in *Syren*'s cutter, did attack a ship's boat crowded with Tripolitans near *Philadelphia* during the boarding attack. The Americans captured the spar deck and gun deck of *Philadelphia* in just ten minutes. It is hard to imagine how a boat could have been lowered from *Philadelphia* given the short period of time available to the frigate's Tripolitan crew. It takes a coordinated effort by group to lower a boat. Decatur's men did not give *Philadelphia*'s crew much opportunity to organize an effort to lower a boat, much less man it.

It seems more likely that the boat attacked by the Americans was the boat lowered from *Philadelphia* to pass a line to Anderson's boat. That boat had to be somewhere, and all accounts agree that Anderson's men attacked one ship's boat and the men swimming to shore after jumping off the frigate. The crew of the boat lowered from *Philadelphia* had no motivation to rush back on *Philadelphia* until *Intrepid* was tied up to the frigate. They could get back onboard *Philadelphia* and be sent to join the men pulling the ketch to the frigate. Or they could just rest on their oars for a while, until the officer-of-the-watch remembered he had a boatful of sailors idling alongside the frigate.

CONCLUSION

With the destruction of *Philadelphia*, the war against the Barbary States tipped in favor of the United States. Until peace was concluded in June 1805, Yusuf Karamanli was forced to stand on the defensive, and he lost more than he gained. In exchange for a payment of $60,000, he released all prisoners, including those captured when *Philadelphia* surrendered in October 1803. Tripoli forfeited receipt of any future annual payment in the treaty, which left it in a worse position than prior to the war – when the United States paid an annual tribute. The $60,000 was significantly less than Tripoli would have received from the United States during the two years of warfare.

Decatur became a national hero because of the raid. On Preble's recommendation, Decatur was promoted to full captain by Congress. Capable and competent lieutenants like Stewart, Hull, and Porter – who had been senior to Decatur – found that he jumped over them in the ranks. Decatur's promotion caused remarkably little public hostility, however, regardless of what private resentments might have been felt.

All of the other officers who participated in the raid, including Stewart, did benefit. They were marked as rising stars, capable men deserving of consideration. Except for Jonathan Thorn – killed while on leave of absence between the Second Barbary War and the War of 1812 – all had been promoted to at least commander by the start of the War of 1812. Stewart joined Decatur as a captain in 1806, promoted due to his outstanding performance throughout the entire Second Barbary War.

Nor was Salvatore Catalano forgotten. Congress conferred US citizenship upon him for his part in the raid. A more concrete reward came from the US Navy, which awarded him a master's warrant – the highest non-commissioned rank in the service. He remained in the US Navy until his death in 1846, having moved to Washington DC in 1806.

Ironically, in view of his role in the raid's success, Catalano is one of the few leaders of the raid not to be honored by having a US Navy warship named after him. In World War II, a flotilla could have been assembled from the destroyers named after participants. Every lieutenant – except for Joseph

JUNE 1805

Peace between the US and the Barbary States concluded

Bainbridge, overshadowed by older brother William and cursed with a dismal post-Barbary War career – was so honored. Even Surgeon's Mate Lewis Heerman merited a namesake destroyer, as did the majority of the midshipmen participating. Of the midshipmen, Macdonough would go on to command the victorious American flotilla at the battle of Lake Champlain during the War of 1812, and Charles Morris would serve as first lieutenant of *Constitution* during its duel with HMS *Guerrieré*.

The officers of *Philadelphia* also had successful careers following their release. William Bainbridge expiated a record of being the only US Navy officer to surrender three ships by capturing HMS *Java* in a frigate duel during the War of 1812. Porter commanded *Essex* on its epic cruise to the South Pacific during that war. Jacob Jones as a master-commandant captured the brig HMS *Dolphin* and sloop-of-war HMS *Frolic* in the same conflict.

Preble was one of the major reasons that Karamanli eventually concluded an unfavorable peace. He kept up the pressure on Tripoli throughout his tenure as commodore of the Mediterranean Squadron. He led attacks on Tripoli in July, August, and September of 1804. The first set of attacks in July tested Tripoli's defenses. It was followed in August by a massive assault by the US Navy, which included a bombardment of the port with both the 24-pdr guns of the frigates *Constitution* and *President*, and 13in mortars launched from bomb ketches. *President*, a sister ship to *Constitution*, had been dispatched from America after *Philadelphia*'s loss, and the ketches had been lent to the United States by the Kingdom of the Two Sicilies. The bombardment cost Tripoli much of the naval force guarding the port and caused great damage to the city and its fortification. It led to an initial peace offer by Karamanli, but Preble found the terms unacceptable. Preble continued pounding Tripoli for the rest of August, but failed to force Karamanli to offer better terms.

On August 4, 1804, Preble's squadron bombarded Tripoli. *Enterprise* is the schooner on the left of the column of ships at the rear. *Syren* is fourth from the left. (USNH&HC)

One consequence of Decatur's raid was that it encouraged other junior officers to seek promotion through bold action. Often these men lacked Decatur's ability to determine the line that separated audacity from foolhardiness. So it proved in September. Lieutenant Richard Somers approached Preble with a fresh scheme to use *Intrepid*. Somers proposed fitting out the ketch as a fireship. This "floating volcano" would be sailed into Tripoli harbor, and lighted among the various corsair vessels docked there, in the belief that most could be burned.

Preble, wanting to increase pressure on Tripoli, agreed to the attempt. As with Decatur's attack, *Intrepid* was filled with volunteer seamen and eager officers. Yet this raid was less focused and less organized than Decatur's attack. Somers did not take Catalano – or any pilot familiar with Tripoli's harbor – even though the attempt required the ability for *Intrepid*, filled with combustibles and explosives, to bluff its way into port.

On September 5, 1804, *Intrepid* was again used to penetrate Tripoli to attack its navy. This attempt ended badly, with *Intrepid* destroyed in a catastrophic explosion, killing all aboard. (AC)

The result was absolute failure. *Intrepid* was detected as it sailed in, and destroyed in a spectacular explosion, although it remains uncertain what caused the detonation. Some observers argued that *Intrepid* was fired to prevent capture by a Tripolitan gunboat. Others believe the explosion was triggered by a shot from a shore battery. The 13 men aboard *Intrepid* were all killed. The attack illustrates the peril that Decatur faced on his attempt to burn *Philadelphia*. Had his purpose been detected before reaching the frigate, *Intrepid* would likely have been destroyed in an identical manner six months earlier.

Preble was relieved by James Barron later that fall. He returned to the United States in winter 1805, and was honored by Congress for his Mediterranean accomplishments with a medal in March 1806. Ill health forced his retirement in 1806, and he died in August 1807.

FURTHER READING

Although much has been written about the Barbary Wars, this is to the best of my knowledge the first non-fiction book to focus exclusively on the raid to burn the *Philadelphia*. This does not mean that there is any shortage of published material about the raid. Accounts of it were perennial favorites in the action-adventure stories popular in the late 19th century. Additionally, the raid plays an important role in any history of the Barbary Wars – and many have been written.

I prefer first-hand accounts by participants when writing a book like this one. Unfortunately, Stephen Decatur died before committing his memoirs to paper. Of the other officers aboard *Intrepid*, only Charles Morris wrote an autobiography that reported experiences during the raid. This work was published posthumously in the 1880s, and has been reprinted by Naval Institute Press in 2002. Other first-hand reports of the action can be found in *Naval Documents Relating to the United States' Wars With the Barbary Powers*, a six-volume set that collects reports created during the Barbary Wars. Volume III covers the burning of *Philadelphia* and contains the reports submitted by various officers. It includes affidavits and statements created two decades after the raid by participants. These were collected by Susan Decatur, Stephen's widow. Impoverished after his death, she wanted Congress to award prize money for *Philadelphia*'s capture. If Decatur could have cut *Philadelphia* out of Tripoli, but was prevented from doing so by Preble's orders, then his widow was entitled to Decatur's share of the prize money. Since the sympathies of Stephen Decatur's colleagues lay with Susan, virtually all came to the improbable conclusion that the only thing preventing *Philadelphia*'s restoration to the US Navy was the pesky orders issued by Preble. Other than that inaccuracy, these statements provide a marvelous window into the raid.

An account of the Barbary Wars that is still valuable despite its age is Garner Allen's *Our Navy and the Barbary Corsairs*. Two other books that I used were *Dawn Like Thunder: The Barbary Wars and the Birth of The American Navy* by Glenn Tucker, and *Our Country, Right or Wrong: The*

The Tripoli Monument at the US Naval Academy. Brought to the United States from Italy in 1806, it commemorates the Navy's personnel that fought the Second Barbary War. (LOC)

Life of Stephen Decatur, by Leonard Guttridge. Edwin Hoyt, a prolific author of naval books, did write a novel about the raid, *Hellfire In Tripoli*, part of a trilogy of adventure fiction centered on the life of Stephen Decatur. It is out of print, but may be found in used bookstores.

Books

Allen, Garner W., *Our Navy and the Barbary Corsairs*, Houghton Mifflin, New York (1905)

Guttridge, Leonard, *Our Country, Right or Wrong: The Life of Stephen Decatur*, Forge Books, New York (2006)

Commodore Preble's
medal. (AC)

Knox, Dudley (ed.), *Naval Documents Relating to the United States' Wars With the Barbary Powers*, 6 volumes, US Government Printing Office, Washington DC (1939–44)

Knox, Dudley (ed.), *Register Of Officer Personnel, United States Navy And Marine Corps and Ship's Data 1801–1807*, US Government Printing Office, Washington DC (1945)

Morris, Charles, *Autobiography of Commodore Charles Morris*, USN, Naval Institute Press, Annapolis, MD (2002)

Tucker, Glenn, *Dawn Like Thunder: The Barbary Wars and the Birth of The American Navy*, Bobs-Merrill, New York (1963)

GLOSSARY

Beating: Sailing with the wind ahead of the ship. Most square-rigged ships could tack no closer than 67 degrees from the direction the wind was blowing, by hauling their yards as far forward as possible. Fore-and-aft rigs could sail closer to the wind, but reaching a position dead to windward required a ship to follow a zig-zag course.

Berth deck: The deck below the gun deck on an American frigate, where the crew sleeps.

Bowsprit: A spar projecting forward from the bow of the ship, to which the stays on the lower sections of the foremast attach.

Brig: A two-masted square-rigged ship with a foremast and mainmast, where the aftermost mast is larger than the foremast.

Broadside: All of the guns on one side of a ship. Firing a broadside involves firing all of those guns either together or at closely spaced intervals.

Carronade: A short-barreled smoothbore gun, mounted on a slide rather than a carriage.

Course: The lowest square sail on a mast, hung from a spar set on the lower mast.

Fore-and-aft sails: Triangular and trapezoidal sails that were rigged parallel to the length of the ship. The sails set on the stays that supported the masts were called staysails or jibsails (if they were on the jib stays). The sail set on a gaff and boom attached behind the mizzenmast was called the gaff, spanker, or spencer sail, depending on the navy, period, and rig. Fore-and-aft sails were used to help steer the ship, and when beating into the wind.

Forecastle: A raised platform at the front of the ship generally used to manage the anchors and foremast and to provide protection from a head sea.

Foremast: On a full-rigged ship, or a brig, the foremost mast.

Frigate: A sailing warship with one full gun deck and additional guns mounted on the forecastle and quarterdeck. A warship with a full gun deck and additional guns only mounted on the quarterdeck is sometimes called a jackass frigate.

Gun deck: Deck on an American frigate or sloop-of-war carrying the main battery of guns. (Considered the upper deck of the ship, despite the spar deck above it.) A ship-of-the-line or two-decker will have more than one gun deck. These are identified by their position – upper, lower, or middle (if there are three gun decks).

Jib boom: A pole or spar extending from the bowsprit.

Jib sails: Triangular sails hung from stays running from the upper foremasts to the jib boom. Used to help steer the ship.

Ketch: A two-masted square-rigged ship with a mainmast and mizzenmast.

Larboard: The left side of the ship, when looking forward. Now called port.

Leeward: The side opposite to the direction of the wind.

Mainmast: Generally the mast closest to the center of the ship. Generally it is also the largest mast.

Mizzenmast: The aftermost mast on a ship with two or three masts when it is the smallest mast. (If the after mast is larger – as on a brig – the after mast is the mainmast.)

Orlop: A set of platforms below the berth deck, but above the bottom of the ship, used to carry supplies and house personnel (generally warrant officers).

Platform: A partial deck on a ship.

Polacre: A three-masted Mediterranean ship, generally with a fine hull and three square-rigged pole masts.

Quarterdeck: A partial deck above the main or gun deck where the navigation and operation of the ship is managed. Generally the quarterdeck starts between the mainmast and the mizzenmast.

Running: Sailing with the wind directly behind you. It is the easiest way to sail a square-rigged ship, but slower than broad reaching, because the after sails obscure sails mounted on masts ahead of them.

Ship-of-the-line: A ship-rigged warship strong enough to stand in the line of battle, with at least two full gun decks and additional guns on the quarterdeck and forecastle. Ships-of-the-line mounted 64 to 140 guns.

Ship-rigged: A ship with at least three masts, all carrying square sails, is said to be ship-rigged.

Shroud: A line running from the sides of the ship to the top of the lower mast, or from the mast top platform or crosstrees to the top of the section of the mast. Used to guy the mast.

Sloop-of-war: A warship with guns mounted only on the gun deck. Three-masted sloops-of-war are often called ship-sloops, and two-masted sloops-of-war are often called brig-sloops. Occasionally a sloop-of-war has additional guns mounted on the quarterdeck. These are also referred to as "post" ships or jackass frigates.

Spanker, spencer, or mizzen gaffsail: A trapezoidal sail mounted aft of the mizzenmast, used to help handle the ship. Spankers and spencers have booms holding the bottom of the sail. Gaffsails often do not. These are called "loose-footed" gaffs.

Spar deck: A flush deck on an American frigate consisting of the forecastle, quarterdeck, and the gangways connecting the two. Generally there is an opening amidships spanned by skids on which the spare spars and ship's boats are kept.

Squaresail: Four-sided sails, occasionally square but more often trapezoidal, set on spars and perpendicular to the length of the ship. American frigates generally mounted five, and sometimes six, sails on their masts. From lowest to highest were the course, topsail, topgallant, royal, skysail, and moonsail or hope-in-heaven. (The name of the sixth sail varied widely.)

Starboard: The right side of the ship when looking forward.

Stay: A line running from the top of a mast segment to either the side of the ship or forward to the next mast ahead or the bowsprit and jib boom. The stays that run forward are called stays. The ones running to the sides of the ship behind the mast to which it is attached are called backstays.

Tack: (In reference to a maneuver.) To tack a ship is to turn it into the wind such that the bow of the ship moves across the direction from which the wind is blowing.

Tack: (In reference to a course being steered.) A ship is said to be on a starboard tack if the wind is coming from the right side of ship. It is on a larboard (or port) if the wind is coming from the left side of the ship.

Topgallant sail: The sail above the topsail. During this period it was carried on a separate mast, called a topgallant mast, attached to the top of the topmast.

Topsail: The sail on a mast above the course. During this period, it was carried on its own section of mast, called the topmast.

Two-decker: A ship-rigged warship with two full gun-decks and additional guns on the quarterdeck and forecastle that is too weak to stand in the line-of-battle. These 44–56-gun warships are miniature ships-of-the-line useful for convoy duty and flagships. They are often confused with frigates because they mount a similar number of guns.

Wear: To turn the ship away from the direction the wind is blowing. This puts less strain on the masts and rigging than tacking (turning into the direction of the wind). Now generally called gybing or jibing.

Xebec: A fine-hulled Mediterranean ship, related to a galley. It typically has three lateen-rigged masts, and is capable of moving under sail or oar.

INDEX